WHERE DREAMS ARE BORN

nonzero\architecture
works
2003–2019

Peter Grueneisen

WHERE DREAMS ARE BORN

nonzero\architecture
works
2003–2019

Michael Webb, Editor

Introduction by
Sam Lubell

Conversations with
Hans Zimmer,
Bruce Botnick,
Brian Riordan,
Thomas Small,
Paul Lieberstein and
Janine Poreba,
Craig Hodgetts

Photography by
Julius Shulman,
Juergen Nogai,
Edward Colver,
Taiyo Watanabe,
et al.

Birkhäuser Basel

CONTENTS

"The founders of game theory ... made a basic distinction between 'zero-sum' games and 'non-zero-sum' games. In zero-sum games, the fortunes of the players are inversely related. In tennis, in chess, in boxing, one contestant's gain is the other's loss. In non-zero-sum games, one player's gain needn't be bad news for the other(s). Indeed, in highly non-zero-sum games the players' interests overlap entirely."

Robert Wright, *NONZERO: The Logic of Human Destiny,* New York: Pantheon Books, 2000

PREFACE

nonzero\architecture was started thirty years ago in the Mid-City area of Los Angeles as studio bau:ton. Due to the partners' mutual interests and the rarity of projects at that recessionary time, much of the initial work was focused on small music recording studios. Music and film were influential touchstones for the young and curious team. From the beginning, the company's initial name, a play on the German words for building and sound, hinted at that passion. It allowed the practice to form, grow, restructure itself, and to immerse itself in a specific program. Projects for music eventually expanded to include related work in film and television and other media. Both the size and scope of projects and the office grew over the years. Working with musicians, composers, audio engineers, filmmakers, and many others made for a very satisfying and stimulating experience. The opportunities we have been given within such a unique field have been central to our work.

But the intention always was to build a practice that concerned itself with every aspect of architecture and lived up to the time-tested model of the architect as a generalist and master builder. From the very beginning, we tried to stay broad-based in our interests and to continue exploring other building types. Arts-related projects of any kind, residential and commercial work, have always been very important to us, as have buildings for education and for entertainment.

Our name has since changed to nonzero\architecture, referring to nonzero-sum games – a concept we found fitting for a discipline that should benefit everyone involved and is not supposed to result in winners and losers. The name is more open-ended and less confining; the goal of this new book then is to place the work within a broader context, to find the common threads that run through it.

In our mind, construction is closely related to architecture, and over the years we have explored various models of integrated project delivery. Architect-led design-build has turned out to be the most effective approach for us, for the builders, and most importantly, for the owners of our projects.

It is these owners who have empowered us and given us the opportunities to continue what we do. We are grateful to each and every one of them – individuals, families, companies of all sizes, institutions, governmental agencies. We wouldn't be here without them. Thank you all!

We wouldn't be able to function without our many dedicated collaborators over the years, our talented team in the office and in the field, or without our trusted engineering and design consultants. Our heartfelt thanks go to all of them as well.

This is our second book, published more than sixteen years after the first one appeared. That first book, studio bau:ton's *Soundspace – Architecture for Sound and Vision,* was focused on a particular niche. This time, we are trying to find common ground in a wider arena and to establish an overarching theme for all kinds of endeavors. We are grateful that the same excellent publisher in Basel, Switzerland, has again given us the opportunity to illustrate our process and some of the resulting projects. Thanks to Annette Gref and Birkhäuser for their patience and guidance with both books over so many years.

We owe a debt of gratitude to our editor Michael Webb, who allowed us to benefit from his lengthy experience with design and architecture books. He helped us with this one in so many ways, including by guiding many of the conversations in this book. Thank you to Sam Lubell for writing an insightful introduction; we were so glad you agreed to do it when we first started this project five years ago.

We are also indebted to the inspiring group of people who were willing to talk to us about different aspects of this book. Thanks to the musical genius Hans Zimmer, to the wonderful engineer and producer Bruce Botnick, to the remarkable engineer and entrepreneur Brian Riordan, to the indefatigable arts doyen and former mayor of Culver City Thomas Small, to our very kind, talented and funny friends and neighbors Paul Lieberstein and Janine Poreba; and to the brilliant architect, writer and teacher Craig Hodgetts.

Thank you to David Goggin, aka Mr. Bonzai, our friend of many years, who knows everyone and everything in music and the industry, for conducting some of these conversations.

We are grateful to the photographers who have contributed their images to this book: the late great Julius Shulman; his photographic partner Juergen Nogai, who captured many projects for us; Edward Colver; Taiyo Watanabe and all the others. Thank you!

Lastly I want to thank my family – my beautiful wife of a third of a century, whose energy and dedication makes all of us look like slackers and who is the truest embodiment of the saying that you can make your dreams come true, if only you set your mind to it, and our two talented and lovely daughters, who are still the greatest things we ever made. Whether working with us on a daily basis in the office, or letting us dabble on their own homes, thank you both for sticking around. You all are my truest inspiration!

Dreams are what inspire people to build homes for their families, artists to create environments for their art, companies to find space to realize their ambitions, and students to find their calling.

Besides these very real dreams and their realization, we create dreams to entertain and to transport us to new worlds and experiences – movies, television, music, games, virtual reality, as well as things still to be invented. Los Angeles has been called the Entertainment Capital of the World and Hollywood is known as the Dream Factory; they are still humming along, as busily as ever.

If we can contribute to the creation of more places where dreams of all kinds are born and made, we will have achieved our goals.

Peter Grueneisen, FAIA
nonzero\architecture

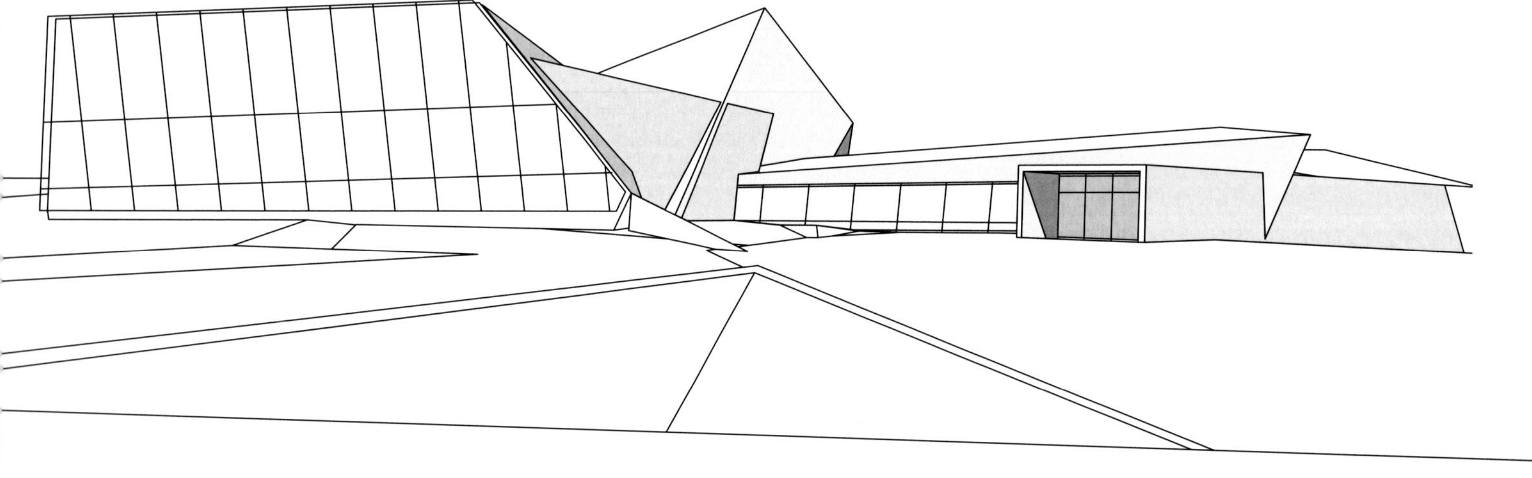

Seracs Helsinki Music Center Competition Entry, 1999

Introduction
Sam Lubell

"Seamless" is how Peter Grueneisen, founder of Santa-Monica-based nonzero\architecture, describes his firm's transition between highly technical entertainment design and luminous residential and commercial architecture. It's a connection that has enriched both sides of the practice in profound ways.

"I don't really distinguish between commercial and residential work," he says. "I look at what's needed, and what works."

Working in Los Angeles, the entertainment capital of the world, nonzero gives its work of all types an appropriately heightened sense of drama and originality, even a cinematic quality. But these are not stage sets. These private spectacles are wholly practical and contain a profoundly human sense of proportion, comfort, and gentleness.

While Grueneisen has become a leader in a highly specialized field – conversant in everything from psycho-acoustics to sound absorption – he doesn't get sucked into the vortex of technical minutiae.

"You can limit your approach to the basic human issues," he says. "It's better to look at the essentials." Art, architecture, and technology all work together, like varying elements of a musical composition. "None can stand alone."

Grueneisen's training helped him draw from both sides of the architectural spectrum. Studying architectural engineering in Biel, Switzerland and working for five years at Swiss-based ARB, he became versed in a rational, modernist approach – although the highly respected firm did at times "engage in some rule breaking," employing some unorthodox spatial and material experiments. From there he jumped to SCI-Arc, where everything was unorthodox, studying under Wolf Prix, and developing a taste for formal complexity.

His ability to maintain restraint in the face of strict parameters, along with a love for unusual, fractured surfaces, played perfectly in the architecture of recording studios. Here clients demand strict technical specifications, but angled walls and curved ceilings are often necessary due to acoustics.

"In this particular program it's not a formal exercise," he explains.

One of the first was Bad Animals Studio in Seattle, where shipbuilders were brought on to custom bend plywood ceiling panels, and angled and free-floating wood elements served both acoustical and psychological functions.

"It's a multi-sensory thing. You're trying to do something for sound, but it's also about the environment. It has to be motivating so you feel creative, but at the same time you don't want to be overwhelming so people get sidetracked. There are moments of exuberance and simplicity," he says.

Something clicked, and Grueneisen's training and talents kicked into high gear. From there he and nonzero, earlier operating as studio bau:ton, have tackled an immense number of music, television, and film production studios for composition, recording, and editing. Rather than developing a strict formal style, like a traditional modernist or even a Wolf Prix, the firm's architecture is always informed by its approach, and by the ultimate function of the space.

Design commonalities include a refreshing exuberance, a sense of tasteful and functional restraint, and a welcoming feeling of comfort. Outside of the necessarily boxed-in studios, public spaces – entries, receptions, hallways – are spacious and filled with light and character.

nonzero employs a sense of lightness, a respect for material, and a willingness to perform visual acrobatics, but not overdo it for its own sake. Sculpture and surprise come through custom milled desks, etched canopies, contorted baffles, digitally milled studio walls, and LED panels. Comfort and connection come through roll-up doors, exposed rafters, skylights, and large windows and window walls. Fabric and wood, needed to muffle sound, also provide a sense of intimacy and warmth.

The firm maintains consistent quality by often working as design builder. "We take more control over the process and stay involved longer," said Grueneisen, who has a contractor's license in addition to an architectural one.

Moving into the residential realm, the needs of the clients have been different, but the process of responding to those needs has been very similar.

In a house, the key is to come up with a narrative, to "have an idea of some kind of a story," Grueneisen said. In LA's Crestwood Hills Residence, the main characters were the canyons, the trees, and the ocean. The houses were designed cinematically to make scenes of those elements, employing a giant glass cantilevered volume, large windows, clerestory glazing, skylights, and tropical hardwood cladding, and offsetting them with exposed concrete and meandering pathways through the houses.

nonzero's addition to Richard Neutra's Freedman House in Pacific Palisades embraces its landscape in a similar fashion, with a generous amount of glass and a similar, but unique, language to the original house. A studio for a major recording artist merges residential work with technical, clad in board formed concrete, and fitted with surface panel lighting systems. A remodeled home for David Lynch, used before as a set for the director's film *Lost Highway*, employs triangular cuts and saw-tooth additions to make the grey, stucco-clad mass more in scale with the neighborhood. Lynch was skeptical but eventually agreed that he had to follow a creative impulse the same way he would in one of his movies.

nonzero's connection to – and inspiration from – film and music is especially strong given that most of its clients are involved in those fields. The firm has a constant back and forth with such creative people. Though the practice rarely advertises the fact, it has also designed studios and homes for Dave Matthews, Will Smith, James Newton Howard, John Fogerty, Tetsuya Komuro, Yoshiki, A.R. Rahman, Stevie Wonder, Ice-T, Peter Frampton, and many others. Institutional clients have included Sony Music, DreamWorks Animation, 20th Century Fox, Warner Brothers, and NBC/Universal. Perhaps it's Grueneisen's Swiss modesty, and a little bit of show business non-disclosures, but the fact that he doesn't throw these names in your face reflects his low-key approach, and the importance of carefully composed design and humility over hype and flash.

His goal is to round out the practice with more public work, to have a more profound impact on the common good. Such projects have shown promising starts, but few have come to fruition yet. They include a mixed-use high-rise proposal on the docks of Dublin for U2 that intertwines leaning towers, a floating base, and hanging gardens; a scheme for the Queens Museum that erodes the building's existing shell, drawing the inside out and the outside in to support flexibility and experimentation; a plan for the Helsinki Music Center whose kaleidoscopic form was inspired directly through a digital analysis of Finnish music; and a colorful campus for the Musician's Institute in Hollywood, integrating divergent facilities through fabric structures, bridges, and pedestrian ways. Another example is the American Legion Hollywood Post 43, bringing together the renovation of a historic structure, integrating film technology, and assisting a charitable organization to open up to the public.

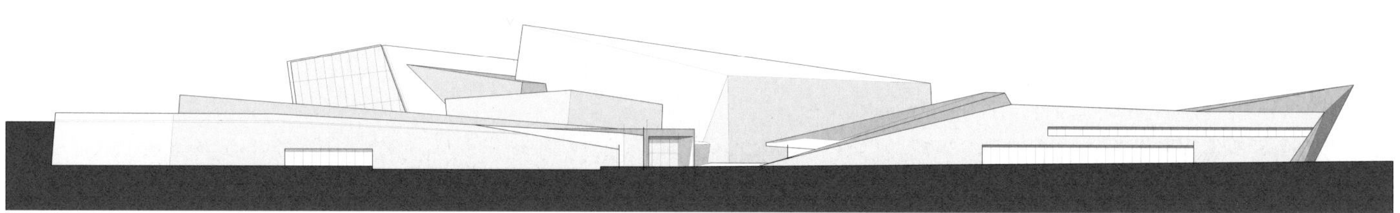

Once again nonzero's core practice travels well from type to type. The sense of ease, comfort, and excitement in these projects can be felt everywhere in the firm's work.

One of nonzero's longest running projects, Hans Zimmer's Remote Control Productions, consists of five new and remodeled buildings along a single street in Santa Monica. Patterns of drilled holes in the metal cladding based on images of Hans's synthesizers, following an earlier glass screen abstracted from a Mozart score, sweep through spaces inside and contribute a feeling of movement and sound. A sense of expanding lightness pervades each space. Entrance areas have exposed trusses, large windows, and skylights, while composing and recording rooms each have their own design, with varying angled fabric-covered walls, screens, and panels.

Here, too, the architecture tells a story. Often it's the story of space and light being informed by sound and image. The spirit of invention coming out of these facilities is both enabled and enhanced by the architecture.

One of nonzero's goals is to make spaces that are inspiring for creativity but not overwhelming. You don't get lost in them; they don't take over. If anything, the work has become more sophisticated over the years. Of course, it's still full of energy and surprises, but "we've learned to strip away some of the superfluous stuff over time," says Grueneisen.

Many of the surprises that show up are what Grueneisen calls "happy accidents". Like turning the pig, cow, sheep, and chicken logos for the firm The Farm into acoustic walls. Or using a client's connection to the lumber business as the inspiration for the use of wood and fluorescent strips in Levels Studio in Hollywood to evoke a sense of movement on its busy street outside, and a dynamic sense of rhythm (and even the musical score or a sound meter) inside. Or finding a secret liquor vault in the basement of a Los Feliz home and converting it into a perfect isolation booth.

"You leave yourself open, but you don't force things in the direction that they're not really going," says Grueneisen. "How do you take something that might be a problem and make it interesting?" Such work has to be done carefully. "It's in the back of our minds. It's a spirit; it's not literal," he notes.

It's a combination of elegance, technical proficiency, humanity, and art that is about making effective spaces for people. It's about creating more than what's called for, but not more than is necessary. It's about spontaneity and inspiration. All of these elements are carefully woven into the architecture and the philosophy. To limit the scope of this work to mere "technical" architecture would be to severely minimize its worth, its intention, and its reality.

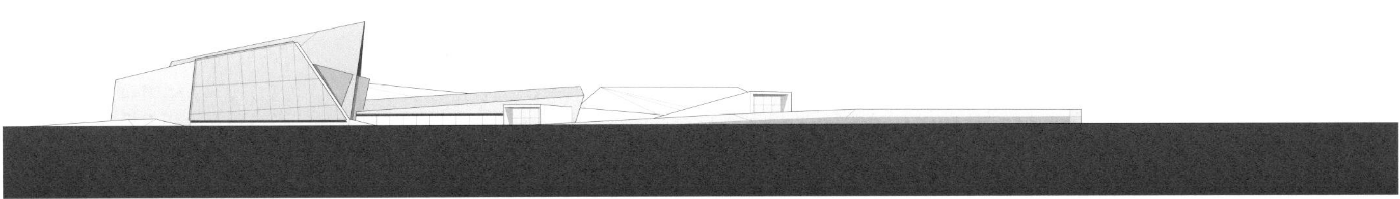

Conversation

Peter Grueneisen with Michael Webb

MW What sparked your interest in architecture?

PG I grew up in a family of craftsmen, going back several generations. My parents owned a wood shop in a small Swiss town, making everything from furniture to kitchens to doors and windows. That environment provided me with a lot of opportunities to build things. I was visiting construction sites at a very young age. Switzerland has a long tradition of valuing and taking pride in craftsmanship; fabricating things was a natural thing to do, especially in the more provincial parts of the country back in the 1960s. But I was less interested in following instructions and plans than in coming up with my own ideas. Once I discovered there was a profession that might just let me do that, I was hooked.

MW Frank Gehry constructed model houses from wood shavings as a child. I'm curious if you felt an urge to build something.

PG Absolutely. I think woodworking had a lot to do with it, and I'm reminded that Peter Zumthor was a carpenter before he became an architect. Growing up, we always made things out of wood, metal, Legos ... whatever we could find.

MW Did you consider other career paths?

PG Not seriously. I was always interested in art, engineering, the environment, even law, politics and diplomacy – but those are all part of architecture, too. I realized later they would all fit in together. But the national universities, like ETH in Zürich or EPFL in Lausanne, seemed like a remote possibility for me; nobody in my immediate family had gone to college, and there wasn't much encouragement to do so. But fortunately there were other ways to get into architecture. So I started by apprenticing as a draftsman, a common path in Switzerland, and then went on to a more local architectural engineering college, visiting lectures at the ETH on the side.

I was fortunate to join ARB in Bern and worked there for over four years. They were a great design office, and they taught me a lot. The mainstream of Swiss modernism drew heavily on the legacy of Le Corbusier, but they were open-minded and were also inspired by others, like Jean Prouvé and Aldo van Eyck. And their interests were broad, outside of architecture itself. One of the partners, Franz Biffiger, is a very accomplished pianist and ran the jazz school in Bern. Others, especially Kurt Aellen, were part of the lively and avant-garde arts scene, so I was opened up to ideas I had no exposure to before. Thomas and Peter Keller were both heavily invested in cooperative housing types. Besides all that, there were influences from France, North Africa, the US – all in all a very diverse environment.

MW Did that prompt your move to LA, to study at SCI-Arc?

PG My wife is American, and although we met in Europe, we were thinking of eventually moving to the US. Architecturally, the immediate impetus was a Swiss magazine's special issue on Frank Gehry, which was a revelation to me, though other Swiss architects found him unserious, even scandalous. And a former schoolmate – Peter Maurer, who would later become my business partner – had already taken some classes at SCI-Arc. I also knew their outpost in Vico Morcote, in the Ticino. It seemed to offer a perfect complement to my earlier, technical education, where there wasn't much emphasis on imagination; it was rather detail-oriented, even dogmatic. Getting a foothold there and expanding my horizons was an enlightening experience, both as a student and later as a sometime instructor. Wolf Prix was one of my professors – Austrian radicalism versus Swiss conservatism. But for all the exuberance of Coop-Himmelb(l)au and Frank Gehry, I found that their projects were well thought out, much more than they got credit for. It helped me to get a well-rounded outlook after that.

MW Did that persuade you to stay in LA? Wolf loved it because he could drive a convertible year- round and had a choice of forty radio stations on his car radio.

PG Europeans (and East Coasters) sometimes have a stereotyped picture of LA as tacky – Disneyland and Universal Studios – but that is just the surface, and the more you know the city, the more it grows on you. Seriousness with a bit of fun; Wolf understood that, as I'm sure you do and Reyner Banham did. Now I can't imagine living anywhere else. I set up my office with two partners in 1990, as soon as I had my degree and license. We named it studio bau:ton in reference to building, the Bauhaus, and to sound. The other Peter had worked for someone who did recording studios and, as a good salesman, he was able to get us jobs in that field, even during a recession. Initially, it was a way to get the work, and then it took off. Music, film, the arts always fascinated me, and working on projects for music was very appealing and personal. Not many people felt comfortable doing that kind of work, since it went beyond the normal responsibilities architects are used to. For us that was exciting.

MW Do you tailor each design to the personality of the client as well as the program?

PG Absolutely. The technical requirements are usually fairly familiar. What takes time and effort is responding to the client's ideas and to the overall context. Even slight variables and modifications can change a project completely. That's where it gets interesting, but there are some limits; we think of ourselves as a contemporary practice, and clients come to us knowing what we do, so there is a certain natural selection involved.

MW Are you able to experiment? How does each job inform subsequent work?

PG One of the dangers of working in a specialized field is that the projects tend to be similar. So we try to push things in different directions and experiment, within reason. Sometimes acoustics is a big factor, and there are limitations due to the laws of physics. But much of that cannot be engineered and is based on intuition and rules of thumb; that's where the opportunities are. Sometimes we might have been a little too daring, and had to go back a step. We've learned from experience and are starting to get better at knowing how to balance things.

MW Talk about the relationship between working and living for professional musicians.

PG As in any field, there is a great variety of viewpoints and tastes. We've had clients who are very forward thinking in their art and very traditional in how they want to live and work. Others are very much in

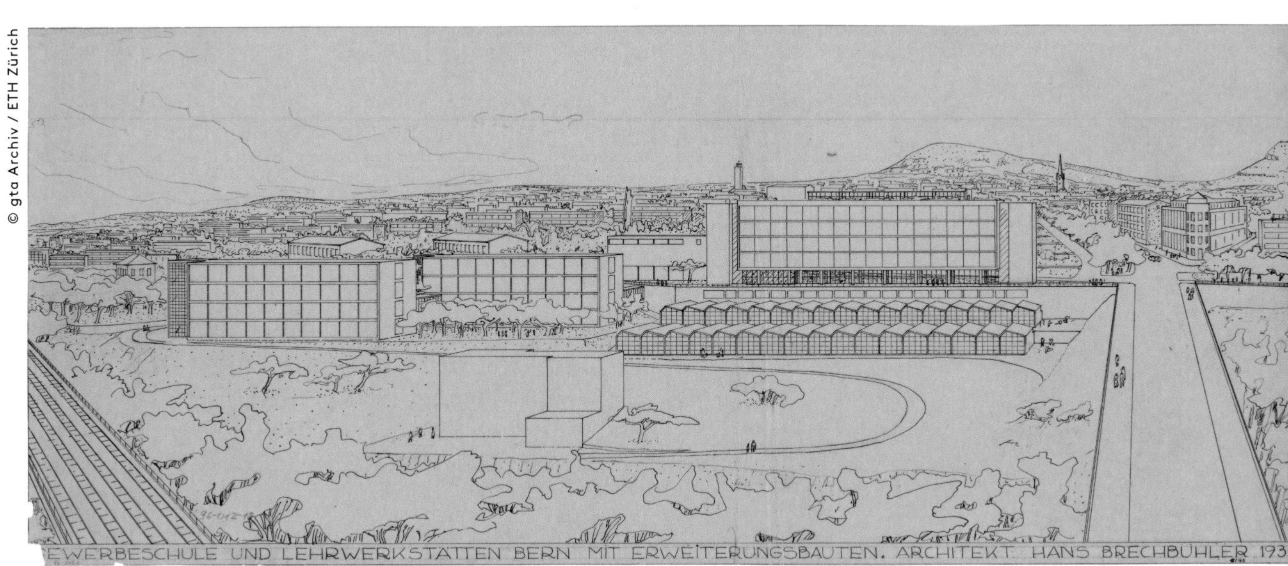

Competition Entry Trade School Bern, ETH Zürich, Hans Brechbühler

© Archiv Atelier 5

Housing development Halen, Architects Atelier 5, Bern

tune with our aesthetic. We've been lucky enough to work with many film composers lately and found their approach very similar to that of architects – working with big teams, relying on a lot of people who participate in the process, yet coming up with the main idea and executing it. They are very good at organizing a project and meeting deadlines while being incredibly creative.

MW Isn't the boundary between living and working disappearing, as people work at home or treat their workplace as an extension of their home? How does that shape your thinking about hybrid spaces?

PG It used to be that making music, movies, or soundtracks required a lot of specialized equipment and companies that provided specialized facilities. That has changed, even in the short time we've been active. Now a lot of things can be done on a laptop or a smartphone, without a crew. Individual creators have more freedom to do things how and where they want. It creates possibilities for us to focus more on the real architectural aspects of a building, beyond the technical requirements. Of course there are still fully professional commercial facilities, but all these programmatic types influence each other.

MW Has your practice evolved dramatically in the past fifteen years?

PG During our initial fifteen-year partnership, we went after every project we could get our hands on, even if it was maybe not a great fit; now we've become more selective, focusing on what we do best, and letting clients come to us. We've downsized and streamlined the office, making it more efficient. Computers allow us to do a lot more with fewer people while expanding our range formally and by building type.

MW When and why did you change the name of the firm to nonzero\architecture?

PG We wanted to broaden our scope, and also went from being a partnership to a single-owner office in 2005. The old name was focused on a particular building type, and we wanted to expand outwards, without losing the expertise in that market. studio bau:ton is still there as a brand for those specific projects. The new name was inspired by a book, *Nonzero – The Logic of Human Destiny* (by Robert Wright), a term from game theory. The math behind it is beyond my comprehension, but the concept is very appealing. It's the opposite of a zero-sum game, where one contestant wins and the other loses. Architecture is always a balancing act, trying to satisfy many different interests, and ideally everyone wins. I thought it was a perfect metaphor. A recent problem is that it can be confused as being the opposite of net zero, which couldn't be

Housing development Merzenacker. Architects Arbeitsgruppe ARB, Bern

farther from the truth; making a net-zero building is a highly nonzero-sum game. We are very interested in that.

MW How many people are working with you now?

PG Currently about eight in the architecture office, but we also have our construction team. Architect-led design-build has been a game changer for us. It allows us to be more involved in the construction process and has been very well received by our clients. It is closer to the European model and the idea of the "master builder".

MW As a leader in your field, are you impatient to explore new ground and on a larger scale?

PG Many of our current projects are very private, but the ideas behind them are scalable for more public venues. In some ways we have done things backwards. We got fairly successful early on and then maybe coasted along a bit rather than continue to grow in terms of project types. Performance venues, cultural centers, and anything that relates to the arts are very interesting to us now, so that's something we are pursuing. We have a very capable team and we collaborate with other firms if the scale of the project requires it. For example, we designed several projects in Asia, leaving it to a large team there to do the working drawings, engineering, and construction. But, as architects we should also pay attention to such urgent issues as climate change and housing shortages.

MW Would you like to grow the office or remain small and involved in every project?

PG Size is not the most important factor for us. At one point we were about thirty people, and there was some loss of control. But it all depends on the internal organization, the systems in place, and the correct flow of information. It becomes a question of designing your firm as much as you would any project. There are small- to medium-size firms, some of them run by good friends of ours, that have figured out ways to scale up the work and still be in charge of the design while doing excellent work. It certainly is something we aspire to.

Currently we are working on developing all that, trying to come up with a sustainable strategy. The goal is to work on fewer but larger projects, but with all of them being more ambitious and satisfactory to everyone involved. Translating our expertise into more public and institutional arts projects, mixed-use and denser residential buildings would be a natural next step.

1 Live and Create

Residence, Proposal, 2019

e-teepee, 2004

Skyline Hardscape, 2012

Laurel Ridge, 2008

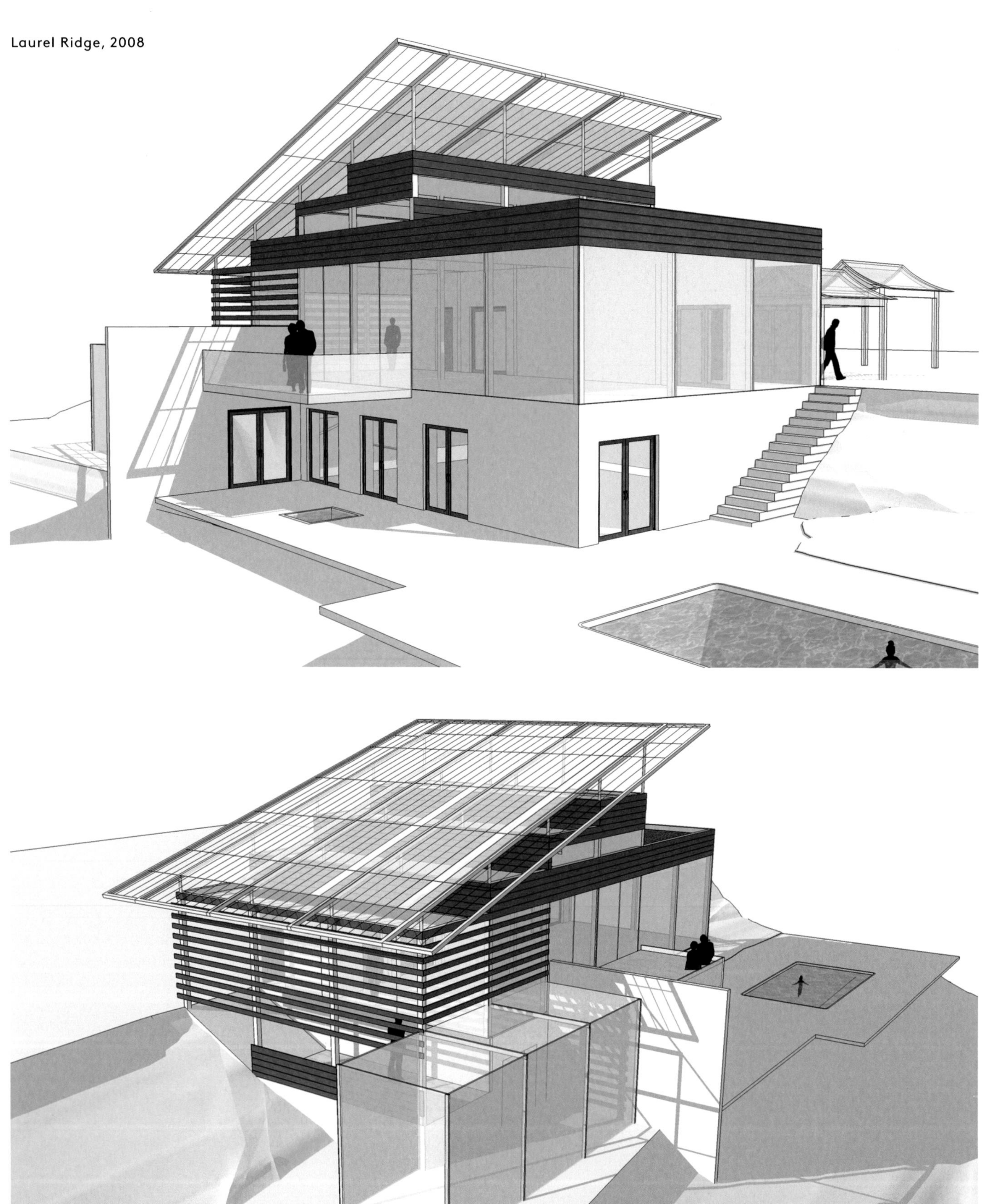

Monmouth, 2016

Malibu, 2015

Dublin Docklands, 2003

Malibu, 2005

Conversation

Paul Lieberstein and Janine Poreba with Peter Grueneisen

PG You have now lived in this same location for almost twenty years, first in your old house, and then in the new one for the last eight years. Your first idea was to add on, but then we built a whole new house from the ground up. Did it make that decision easier knowing that you wanted to both work and raise a family there?

PL We were willing to consider different ways; when we finally realized we could have a house where we could each have an office and really live there, that seemed irresistible. The first idea was to expand in a smaller way, but I guess it was the design, which you showed us first in very conceptual ways, that really attracted us. We really liked the concept of a house wrapped around a glass box, a space that could adapt to different phases of our lives as a family. We didn't want a house that separated us by its design and stuck us in different parts, but one that actually kept us together. So it was a great marriage between the concept and how we wanted to live.

PG You had worked out of the old house before; so providing studies for each of you was a big priority. You even came up with the idea of having the rotating bookshelf between the living space and the two planned offices, like in the movie *Young Frankenstein*.

PL Yes, I thought of that independent of any concept of function. I always just wanted to have the revolving Abbott and Costello door! But it's interesting; the house evolves in different stages. Right now those are rooms that are used a lot, but not that much for our work. I found my room to be too close to the action for me to actually be working. So I have a downstairs office that was initially going to be a gym and will maybe become a gym again, later on. But it has also become a yoga studio and a playroom, a spillover. Right now it's filled with Legos. The house is adapting and shifting in ways that we didn't expect.

PG Many projects in this chapter include very specialized spaces, aside from their function as houses to live in. But here, the different activities are more integrated.

JP Sometimes we wish we could separate our spaces more from the kids, but they just won't let us! But the separation between the upstairs and downstairs is working; there is a public and private thing going on. This living space is very daytime, and when it gets darker, we go downstairs. And when we have guests, we leave them up here. We just go down there with the kids, and it's almost like a whole other shift.

PL These two study rooms have been part of the great room more than we suspected. The upstairs keeps us all together, and the downstairs spreads us out.

PG So do you sometimes leave the revolving door open?

JP That turned out to be a real thing, I've done that to keep an eye on the kids.

PL It's a lot easier that way; if you don't leave the door open they'll find their way in, but if you leave it open they'll continue to play outside, or at their art table.

JP And these rooms also function quite often as guest rooms. It is like a guest suite, for different groups, almost as a stand-alone unit. Relatives and friends come and stay there for various holidays over the year.

PG You started a family around the time the house was being built. It must have felt like a real beginning, even if it was in the same place you had lived in for a while.

The glass box

JP Everything went together at once, but it also kept things in perspective, because we had a baby. For example, something like choosing doorknobs was really not a big deal, considering everything else. If it had been a different time in our lives, we might have been more involved in the design process, because it is sort of fun to pay attention to the details. But for us it was more – how can we even get a babysitter while we go to the appliance showroom?

PL It definitely was a great reality check, and we didn't get lost in the details of the planning.

JP And we still felt like we continued to grow into it, like it was the start of something. For a while we were just occupying one room, but then, as our daughter found her footing more, the range expanded. Different rooms started having different uses.

PL The house keeps surprising us in that way, it is adapting very interestingly.

PG Paul, you have been instrumental on a very funny and successful TV show, yet the television in your house is placed very discretely and can be hidden easily.

PL I thought a lot about television and I didn't want it to invade. There is always this battle, especially in rooms with fireplaces - how to orient things, towards a fireplace, towards a TV, towards a view? We didn't want a home that was just oriented towards a TV. And this is not a television room, it is really our great room, our living room and we didn't want that to be the focal point. Being able to swing it away was really important.

PG Do you feel the environment at home is an inspiration for your work, or the opposite, a distraction, or maybe both?

JP I love being in my home office, I love tidying it up and getting ready to work there, I wish I had more time to be in there.

PL Working at home is a treat; but it is hard. It is all so close! It is a little bit of both.

JP: We had an idea to go out to the car, park a little ways away and then go downstairs on the outside to go to the office...

PL But it felt so deceptive! I worked downstairs for a few years, but when they started to find me there, I rented an office a few miles away. It will probably just be a couple more years and then I'll be back here again.

PG I imagine as a writer you work in a solitary situation a lot, but when you do comedy, you may need a larger group. Have you had people come here to work?

PL Generally I haven't done that here. But it really depends on the kids' ages and their schedules. Maybe we'll phase into that, I would love to do that someday.

PG Janine, you are now teaching English as a second language, helping people to fulfill their own dreams by become more integrated into society.

JP Yes, I work at home a lot to prepare, grade and that happens all over the house. Depending on the light, the sun. The light is part of the ecosystem here, the house can feel very different at times in different areas.

PG We were thinking of the entrance behind the kitchen box and then how it reveals the view of the great room almost as a cinematic sequence, a narrative.

JP Yes, whenever someone new comes into the house they are struck by it. We still feel it after being away for a while and coming back, we are wondering why we left.

PL I love the way the house is discrete from the front; it does leave some surprises. It still has a sense of a tree house, and the expansive views of the water and trees; but we also seem to find new areas, like the patio outside the master bedroom with the scent of the lemon trees, which we hadn't used much and just recently discovered again.

JP Who said, When you dream about a house you are dreaming about yourself? Is that a common thing? It does ring true in some ways.

Paul and Janine are the owners of the featured Crestwood Hills project and have been the architect's neighbors for the last fifteen years.

Pacific Palisades
Los Angeles, California

This residence was originally designed and built in 1949 by Richard Neutra for the screenwriters Benedict and Nancy Freedman. The small house occupied a large lot on a bluff, was set back from the street, and offered privacy as well as unobstructed ocean views. After some initial modifications by Neutra himself, several additions were designed and built between 1959 and 1988 by different architects.

In the mid-nineties, the first phase of the work presented here was started. It attempted to complete a building that was missing many exterior elements, and to surround the house with structures that screened it from the street, were sympathetic to the original, and fulfilled the contemporary demands of the house. It included the completion of the hardscape around the house, the addition of a garden shed and privacy walls, gates and entrance stairs, garden walls, and landscaping. A reflecting pond by the entrance was added, and the siding was restored to the original stained redwood finish.

From 1999 to 2002, after an ownership change, the second phase – the addition of a second floor with two bedrooms and baths, an enlarged master bath area, and the remodel of the kitchen – were undertaken. An aluminum trellis was added to a patio outside the kitchen, which had been completed in phase one. The additions blended with the original structure, and the basic idea of the open flow between the inside and the outside was maintained and reinforced in all areas.

The historical significance and spatial quality of the existing building were determining factors for the architectural approach for both phases, and were clearly understood and supported by both clients. The early alterations that had been made had changed some of the character of the house. Although they were mostly well integrated into the original, the structure could no longer be considered a pure and pristine Neutra house.

The second phase, with a significant addition of floor space, had the potential to change the character of the house greatly. A conscious decision was made to design the new elements as integral parts of the original structure. Parts of the house were restored to their original state, while new portions attempted to interpret the intent of the original design and to extrapolate the inherent spatial and structural ideas.

The second floor achieves a dynamic on its own, with large window bands and roof overhangs with detailing emulating the original. But despite the significant change in the massing, the final composition is meant to result in an integrated and seamless sense of continuity between the different generations of the building.

The master bathroom extension extends into the rear pool courtyard and intensifies the more urban character of the space with the addition of a horizontal stone wall. The resulting spatial intensity plays off the yard sloping towards the ocean, visible through the transparent and openable living room to the south.

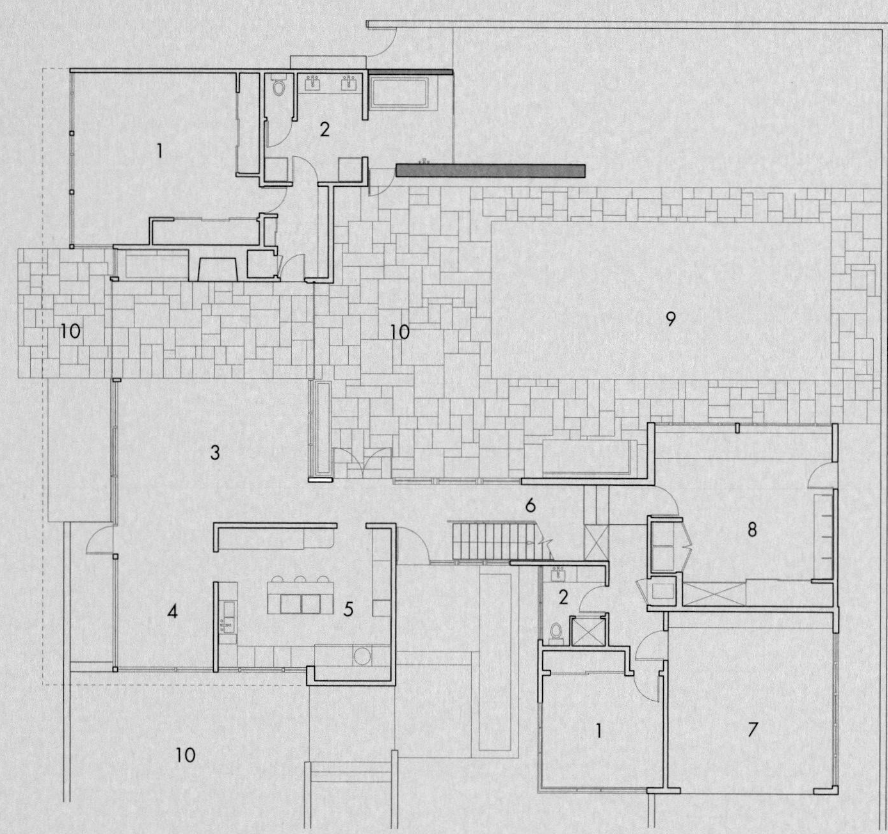

FIRST FLOOR PLAN

1 Bedroom
2 Bathroom
3 Living room
4 Dining
5 Kitchen
6 Gallery
7 Garage
8 Studio
9 Swimming Pool
10 Patio

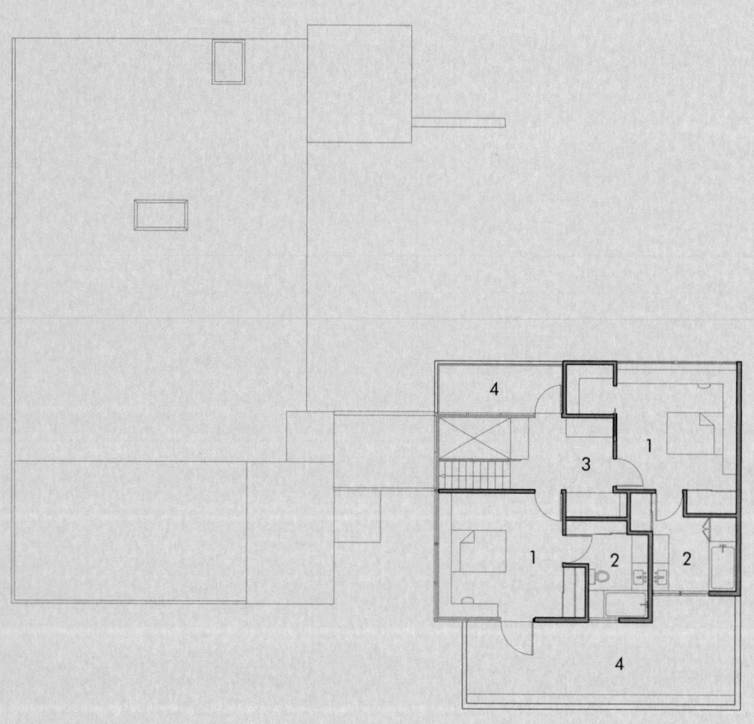

SECOND FLOOR PLAN

1 Bedroom
2 Bathroom
3 Sitting Area
4 Deck

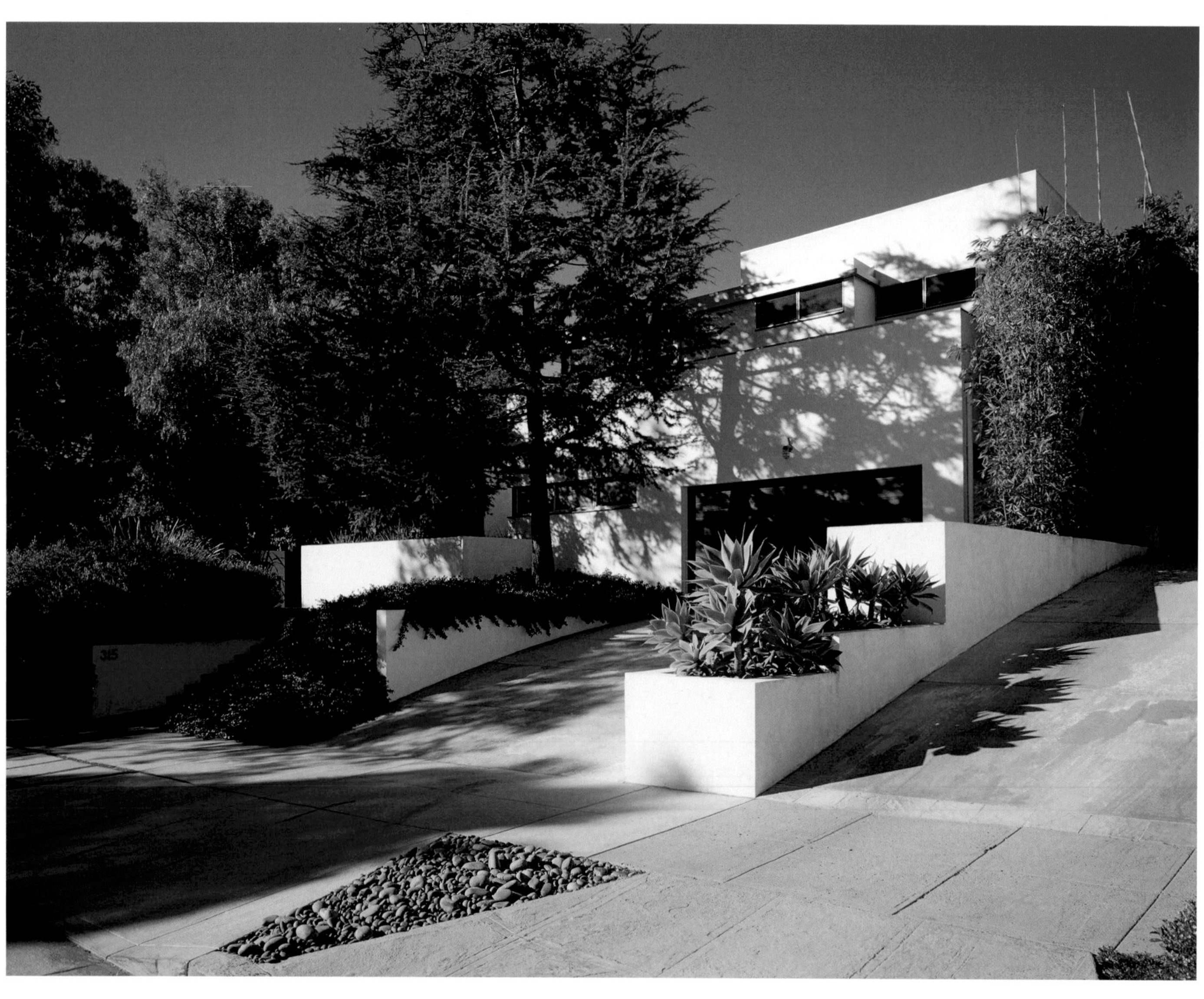
315

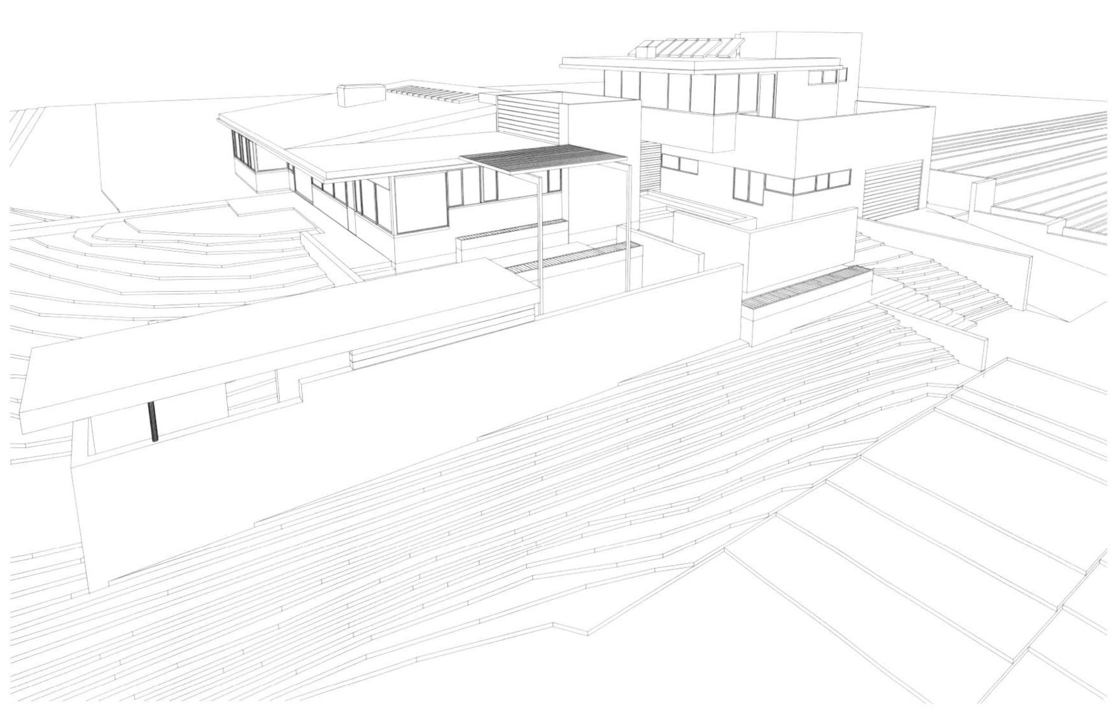

Crestwood Hills
Los Angeles, California

The new single-family residence is located in the historic Crestwood Hills neighborhood, an area with strict regulations enforcing a mid-century ideal of rustic modernism and a collective approach to planning and design. The initial idea to expand an unremarkable 1940s house on the property was soon abandoned in favor of building from the ground up.

The massing concept includes a simple glass volume for the shared living spaces, wrapped around three-dimensionally with a solid band of private rooms that maintain the owner's privacy from the public. The preservation of views and a sensitive approach to the down-slope site dictated a one-story elevation from the street. In keeping with the neighborhood, a low profile and the careful positioning of the volumes makes the relatively large home appear modestly scaled.

The living room, dining room, and kitchen are all placed in the open volume, which extends onto a large deck through folding glass walls. Throughout the house, views of the canyon, the trees, and the distant shoreline are carefully framed for maximum enjoyment as well as privacy.

Closely integrated into the historic surroundings, the ground floor features a typical transparent clerestory above the opaque walls and a floating flat roof with exposed steel beams. The solid exterior walls are clad in wood, contrasting with the large expanses of steel- and aluminum-framed high-performance glass. The desired strong interior-exterior relationships, maximum openness, and a focus on craft and detailing are achieved with a glazed post and beam structure. Built-in mahogany cabinets and shelves, including a rotating shelf wall, help to keep the tall space open and uncluttered while adding warmth to the interior environment.

The lower floor is dedicated to the bedrooms and bathrooms, a private study, and a large, usable, multi-purpose basement space. The exterior patios on this level activate a previously unused hillside and make it more accessible from the house.

The environmentally efficient house features photovoltaic solar panels that shade the deck and allow dappled daylight to filter through. The house is protected from the summer sun with roof overhangs and exterior shades. Natural ventilation is facilitated through the placement of operable windows and folding glass walls to the large deck, along the path of the prevailing breezes. Roof beams from the old house have been repurposed as steps and benches throughout.

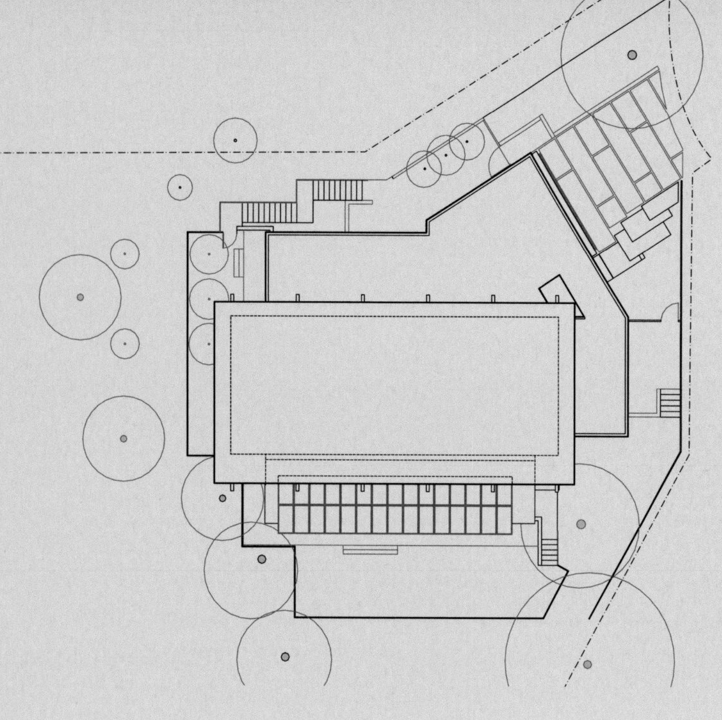

SITE PLAN

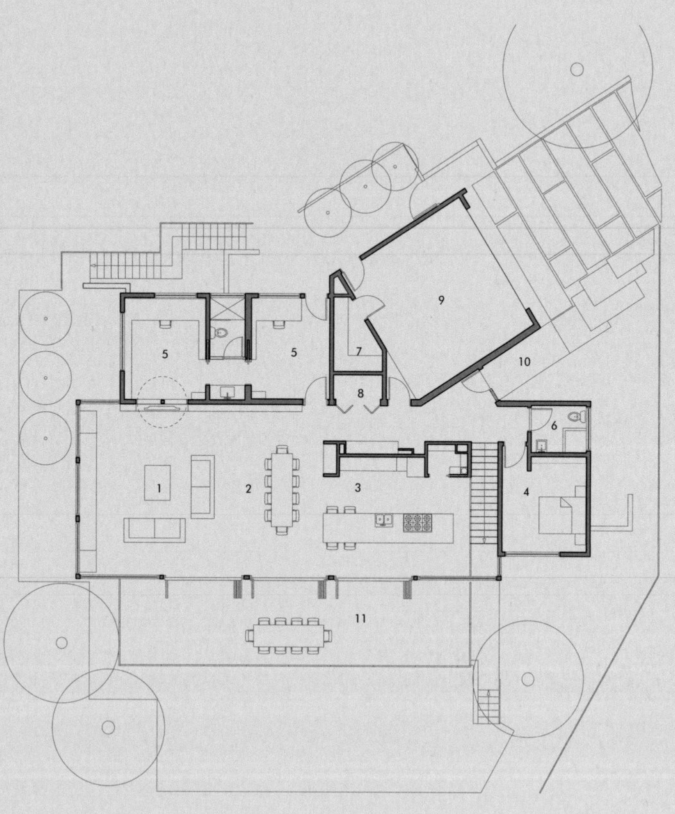

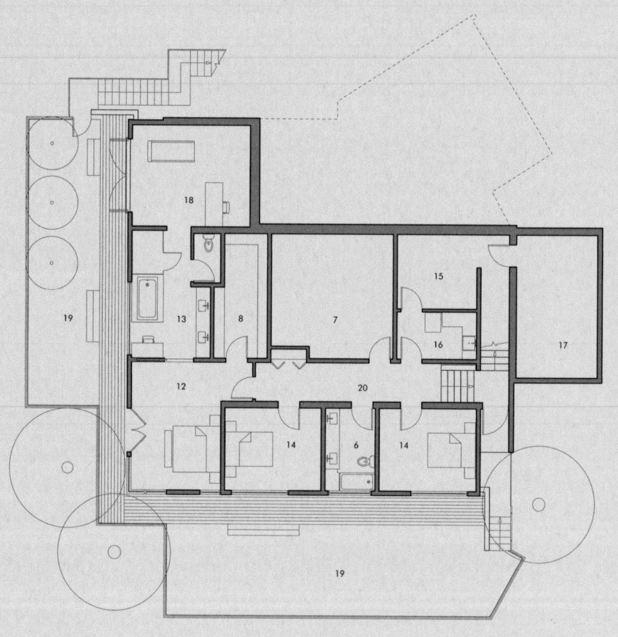

GROUND FLOOR PLAN

1 Living Room
2 Dining Room
3 Kitchen
4 Guest Room
5 Study
6 Bathroom
7 Storage
8 Closet
9 Garage
10 Entry
11 Deck

LOWER FLOOR PLAN

6 Bathroom
7 Storage
8 Closet
12 Master Bedroom
13 Master Bathroom
14 Bedroom
15 Mechanical Room
16 Laundry Room
17 Crawl Space
18 Gym/Rec. Room
19 Lower Yard
20 Hall

MASSING CONCEPT

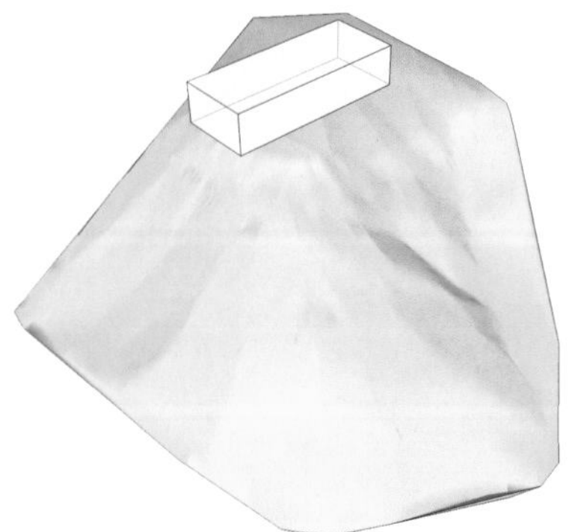

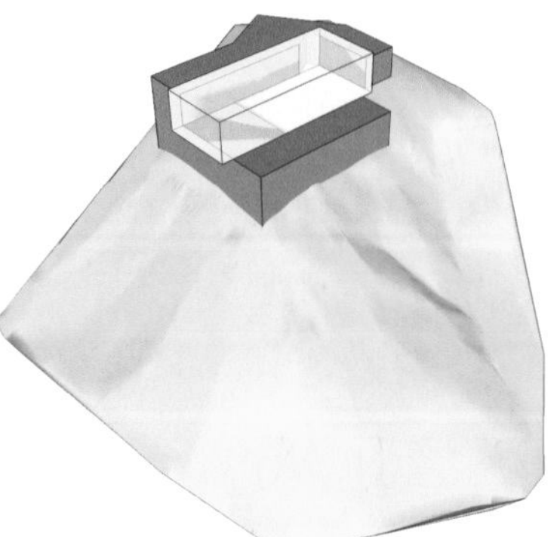

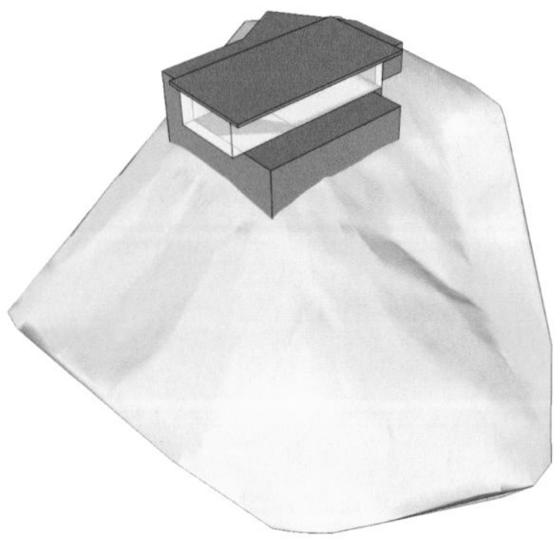

The revolving bookshelf

Mar Vista

Los Angeles, California

The Mar Vista neighborhood, located near the coast, has seen a rebuilding boom over the last decade. The planned new residence is located on a cul-de-sac at the bottom of its hilly edge. The owner, an artist, musician and photographer and a previous client, was looking for a simple and streamlined modern house for himself. While preserving and adding on to the original house was considered, it did not make sense from both a planning and economic standpoint.

Inspired by the LA Case Study houses, the parti consists of two perpendicularly arranged, stacked, rectangular building bars. The ground floor divides the property into a front and back half, while the upper floor runs front to back and creates privacy from the neighboring elevated house to the north.

The street side of the lower floor and the back of the upper volume are mostly closed off, but the facades facing the backyard and the view to the south are entirely glazed.

The living room and the kitchen are placed in the lower volume and are spatially extended into the backyard with its mature trees, for a daily indoor-outdoor experience. The long overhang created by the upper volume creates a covered area that may be enclosed as an additional room in the future.

The upper floor includes a master bedroom, bathrooms, a music and photography studio, and a long open hallway, leading to a large deck. Its walls and ceilings are clad in plywood panels, as is the ceiling on the lower floor. A polished concrete floor on the lower level and concrete tiles upstairs continue the consistent approach to the interior finishes.

The exterior will be finished in smooth stucco at the lower level with a rusted steel rainscreen above. The natural steel will also be used for fencing, and drainage details below are conceived to minimize staining from the weathering process.

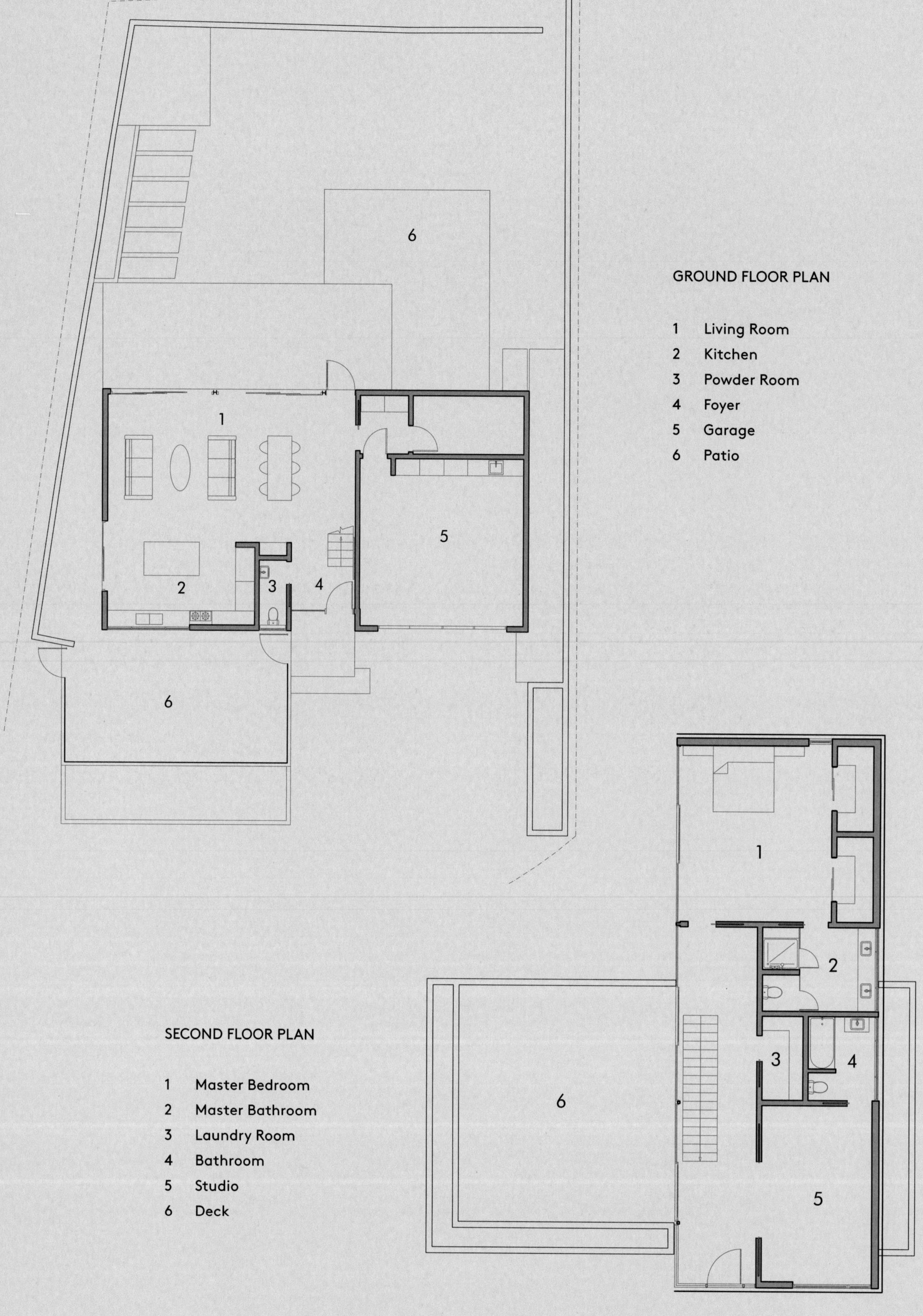

GROUND FLOOR PLAN

1 Living Room
2 Kitchen
3 Powder Room
4 Foyer
5 Garage
6 Patio

SECOND FLOOR PLAN

1 Master Bedroom
2 Master Bathroom
3 Laundry Room
4 Bathroom
5 Studio
6 Deck

Conversation

Thomas Small with Michael Webb

MW Goethe called architecture frozen music; what do you see as the affinities between the two arts?

TS There's been a lot of discussion of that metaphor over many decades, how each discipline has a system and a language with its own rules. The other quote that comes to mind is by Joseph Conrad: "music is the art to which all the others aspire". Wagner believed that musical motifs could be attached to a story or characters. Stravinsky went in the opposite direction, insisting that music was pure and didn't have any programmatic significance. The conjunction of great music and architecture is one of the ultimate experiences that a human being can have. When you are in exactly the right environment you can have a sublime experience – be it the courtyard of a convent in Rome with a spectacular chamber music group, the salon of a palace, the Ojai bandshell surrounded by birds and squirrels, Walt Disney Hall, the Musikverein, or somebody's house. Participating in that process, even from way in the back, has been one of the joys of my life.

MW You made many demands of your architect for this house. How high on the list was musical performance?

TS Very high. Having a creative brief that is clear and direct makes for very successful architecture. We had a limited budget, and we wanted the house to be sustainable, to work as a domestic space for the family and our two Briards, and then there was the music. That created a decision tree: every major and minor element was dropped or considered very carefully if it wasn't in the budget. The prefabricated steel building had many advantages including the huge volume of this great room – 24 feet wide and 26 feet high – with its mix of surfaces, hard and sound-absorbing. It's not the most forgiving acoustic, but for good musicians it's an extraordinary space, providing an intimacy and clarity without the music being too loud.

MW Listeners are seated within 20 feet of the players. Surely, at that distance, it's not such a challenge to ensure good acoustics?

TS Exactly. It's easy to have good sound, although a nine-foot concert grand would overwhelm the space, so we use smaller pianos. It works well for many different kinds of music, and it's a revelation to listen to in a family setting, with neighbors, children, and dogs. It gathers us together in a communal experience where you are at once alone with the music and together with other people – which is even more regenerative in an age of social media.

MW How did you reconcile your detailed brief with your desire to give your architect a wide measure of creative freedom?

TS It was a productive collaboration, very organic. We would both come up with ideas that were within the parameters we had set and bounce them off each other. Most decisions were easy to make. One that took a while was the custom glass balustrade on the ramp that leads up to the second floor and doubles as a gallery for recitals. There are two layers of glass, tempered and laminated, with rice grass between them and clear glass at the top to assure good sightlines. Mostly we employed inexpensive industrial materials, but the glass cost $7,000; that was a challenge and it took us many months to agree. It turned out to be one of our best decisions, for it makes the house by personalizing it.

MW Were you also thinking about the acoustic balance of soft (shredded jeans) and hard (glass)?

Small Residence and music space, Sander Architects

TS When you have a small budget, you are working on the fly; a lot of things are unaffordable, in terms of time and material cost. However there have been many advances in the fifteen years since we started planning this house. Today we could use a computer model to control energy use, test materials and strategies, and plan acoustics. Even so, it turned out pretty well.

MW How important are psycho-acoustics? Is that why this space is so popular with chamber musicians?

TS So many things have to line up for a musical experience to realize its full potential. When I was a kid growing up in the Bay Area, my first exposure to music was with a family who would invite local musicians to play marathon sessions, from 4 pm to midnight. I remember a lavish buffet in one room, kids running in and out, the warmth and civilized quality of it. That's one way to approach psycho-acoustics. There have been many memorable moments in the concerts we've hosted over the past decade. One of them was Ben Johnston, one of the great micro tonal composers, making a rare visit to LA. We premiered his "Amazing Grace" string quartet. Because the melody is so familiar, it's a very accessible piece. The Calder Quartet took it on tour; others followed their lead, and from that night on, the piece entered the standard repertory.

MW You are able to experiment – with your hybrid house, your programming, and the configuration of the audience – and the domesticity of the setting enriches the experience. Have there been any trade-offs between living and listening or have they been mutually reinforcing?

TS There always are. My wife, Joanna, has been so kind and tolerant of my immersion in music over the years. It was good to have a little break from concerts while serving as mayor of Culver City. They take a lot of time and effort to organize, and I have to buy and prepare the food. It's challenging but rewarding. Often the programming is off-the-cuff. Members of the Calder Quartet live close by, and if they want to try out a thorny addition to the repertoire before taking it on tour, they may ask if they can come over next Tuesday night. I then call a few friends, and the quartet will perform for twenty people. They've even played when the house was empty. There's a choral group called Vox Femina, and they staged a benefit as a cabaret, with the singers in the gallery and the audience sitting at small tables. The conjunction of those different groups in Culver City has made it uniquely possible to have them perform here.

MW You've planted a seed, much like the Monday Evening Concerts, which began in an upstairs room of a Schindler house in Silver Lake.

TS You've made me think again about the relationship between great music and architecture. There's a beautiful set of poems by Wallace Stevens that depicts him sitting in a room full of dappled sunlight, reading or writing. He's experiencing the sublime through poetry, alone on a still night – a conduit to the spiritual. Concerts can offer a similar experience of order and beauty in a communal way, a bulwark that allows us to survive our everyday trials. Here, we are a community participating in the music. It lessens the distance that separates players from the audience in a concert hall.

PG You mentioned the value of having a precise brief. We architects sometimes rely on happy accidents, and I wonder if unexpected things happened in the design of this house.

TS Oh, yes. The most interesting one is the impact of this volume, which is like a shoebox turned on its side. The thing we did not anticipate was the experience of walking into this room from the low-ceilinged entrance, which draws on Frank Lloyd Wright's idea of compression and release. We had no idea of the universe this room creates. Lying on this couch as the light changes through the day, I notice how the spaces at the top around my office become ever more mysterious – the structure of the hanging light fixture, the spiral stair and the metal railings, the complex pattern of the window mullions. As the shadows deepen it becomes an infinite space and evokes Piranesi. Even in the bedroom the ceiling is 16 feet, and you can see the moon move by. I wanted a roof deck, but the third-floor balcony is just as dramatic, opening up a view of a mountain you didn't know was there – the art of the unexpected.

PG Technological resources have never been greater, but architects may have become too reliant on experts, rather than drawing on precedent and their own experience. With acoustics, if you understand the basics, you are ninety per cent there. Here, by understanding your personal requirements and the fundamental rules of performance spaces, you've intuitively achieved just the right mix.

Thomas Small is a strong supporter of the arts and architecture and, with his family, the owner of a house designed to host chamber music.

West Valley
Los Angeles, California

The owners of this newly acquired residential property had been looking for a site with enough space for an accessory building to house a personal recording studio as well as a gym and a pool. The upslope flag lot was just wide enough to accommodate a building, with a long driveway for privacy, and to allow for the secondary structure to sit in front of and below the main residence.

Placing the personal studio and production facility for the producer and songwriter husband at the lower level helps create some distance from the house and aids in the soundproofing. The upper level is taken up by the gym, outdoor decks, and a new pool and hot tub for the health-conscious young couple.

The pool level forms a natural transition and mediates the sloping topography between the structures. The new building follows the contours of the hill and driveway, but the main roof creates a countermove by sloping up and opening up to the sky to the east.

The studio consists of a tall, airy, and light-filled recording room, complemented by an equally generous adjacent control and production room. Also included are a private visitor's lounge and a sky-lit awards and art gallery that forms a guided pathway to the main studio entrance.

The live recording space features angular ceilings with integrated color-changing light strips and a faceted and triangulated pegboard wall, both designed to optimize the acoustics in the space. Tall windows offer daylight and views to the greenery outside, but can be closed with automated shades for privacy and a more intimate feel.

The control room has many of the same features and is equipped with a custom-built walnut workstation desk and massive freestanding main speakers. Acoustic diffusers in the rear wall are made from the same wood and are framed by a pair of windows leading to the daylit gallery and entrance hallway.

The mostly white color scheme throughout the building is accented with dark gray fabric panels and a polished concrete floor. The gym above the studio opens up to the deck, and all of its four walls feature large windows. The pegboard recurs here on the ceiling, and the floor is covered in rubber.

Discrete flat screens in wood frames display digital art when not being used as TV and video monitors, contributing to a serene and residential feeling in the building.

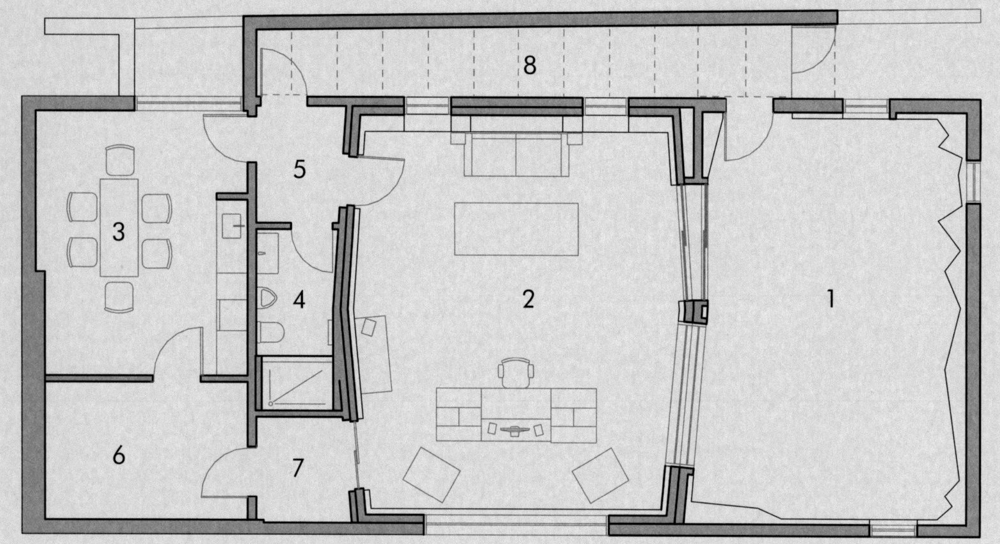

GROUND FLOOR PLAN

1 Studio
2 Control/Mix Room
3 Lounge
4 Bathroom
5 Vestibule
6 Mechanical
7 Equipment
8 Entrance Gallery

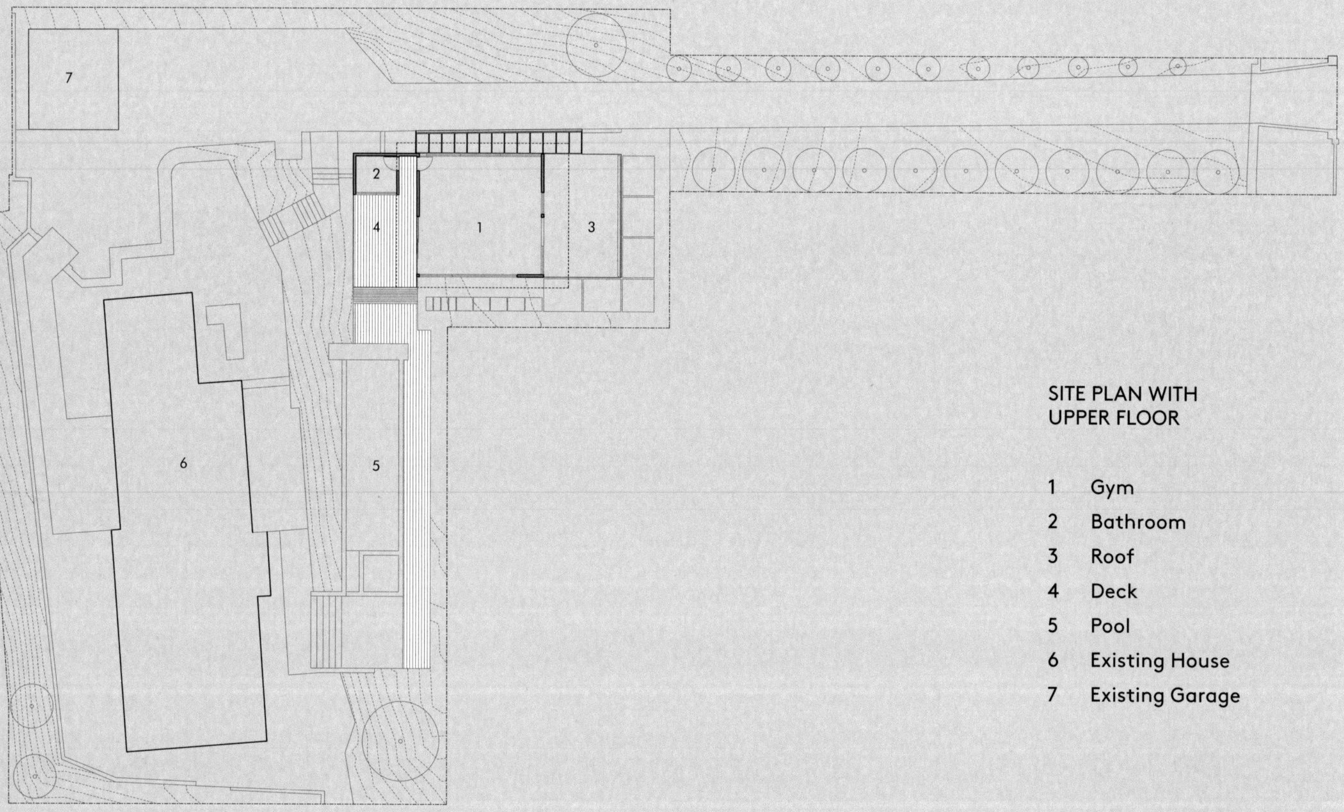

SITE PLAN WITH UPPER FLOOR

1 Gym
2 Bathroom
3 Roof
4 Deck
5 Pool
6 Existing House
7 Existing Garage

The Barn

Malibu, California

When the owners of Windmark Studios acquired a residential property in the Malibu hills, it came with an unfinished structure that had originally been conceived as a horse barn. There were no horses, but to the husband, a singer-songwriter and consummate musician, the empty shell seemed like a perfect location for his personal home studio.

The raw concrete structure, already covered with a tile roof, was sitting unused below the main residence, remote enough for privacy, and with scenic views in all directions. The floor plan had been separated into two main areas, conducive for a studio layout, and the unfinished dirt floor allowed for the installation of wiring conduits and hidden air ducts.

Divided up into a control and writing room and a recording booth, the built-out structure now features a personal studio and creative space. In a departure from the spare aesthetic of most of nonzero's work, the exterior is finished with rough-hewn wood planks and natural stone facing over the poured-in-place concrete walls. Barn door hardware used for shutters and gates allows the building to be shut down completely during the owner's longer absences.

The rustic approach hints at the structure's original purpose and complements the hand-made quality and the warm sound of the vintage recording gear used inside. One of the main elements of the new build-out is the use of repurposed wood, salvaged from the Hollywood Bowl when its bench seating was recently replaced. The wood, which was also milled to make a floor and deck and a built-in seating area, had aged over decades in the iconic outdoor amphitheater. Some of the original carved seat numbers are positioned at the back of the built-in bench. The more rounded boards are used to form acoustically appropriate sound diffusers on the front wall of the space. Having witnessed countless great musical performances, the wood is a perfect symbolic match for this dedicated musician's creative space.

Barn door hardware is used to hang acoustic and privacy panels on the sides of the writing room, allowing complete flexibility to fine-tune the environment. Their fiberglass treatment is covered with hay-colored burlap fabric, similar to the produce sacks used to upholster the seating and pillows. Glass chandeliers add a bohemian touch to the rustic modern interiors and the outside deck.

While located away from city noise and from the house and the neighbors, soundproofing was still taken seriously and thoroughly detailed. The acoustic properties inside the studio were carefully calibrated, making it the owner's favorite creative space, ahead of even his larger Windmark studio.

Just outside the writing room, the deck with its expansive ocean view serves as a relaxation area and as a stage for intimate outdoor concerts for family and friends.

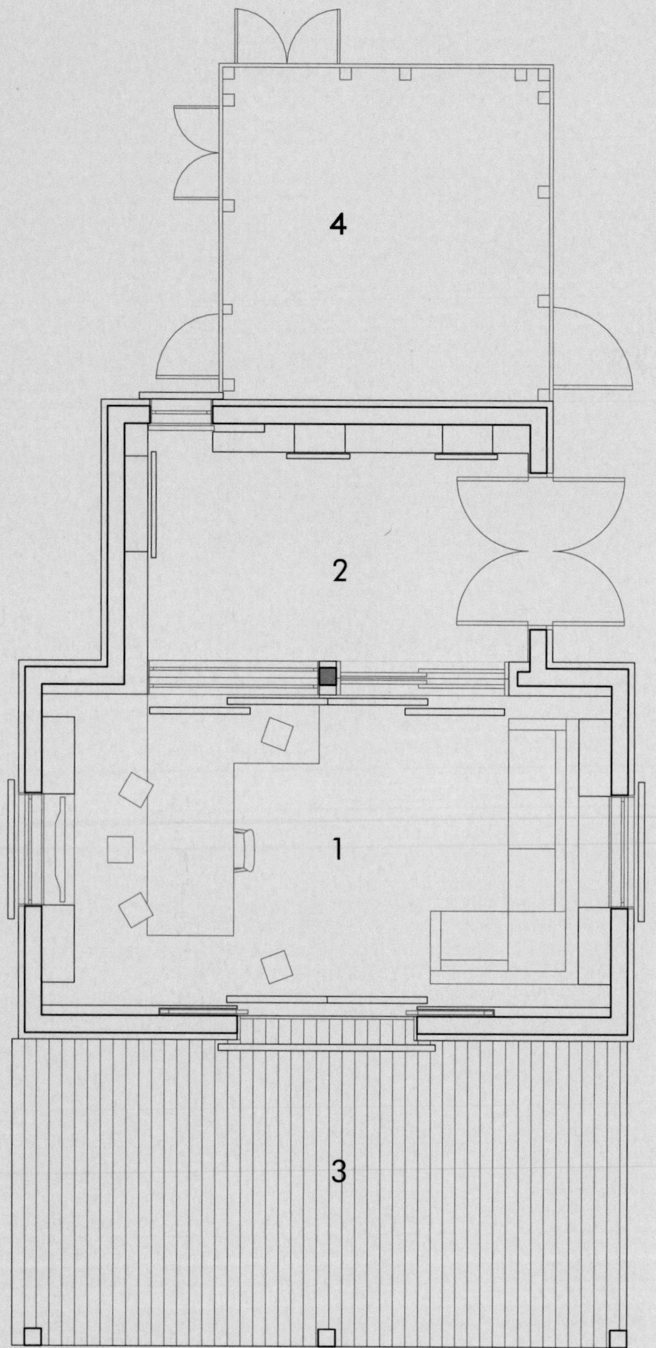

FLOOR PLAN

1 Writing/Control Room
2 Recording Space
3 Stage/Porch
4 Mechanical Yard

MARSHALL
Marshall

Marshall

Marshall

Marshall
BOSE

2 Compose

JNH, 1996

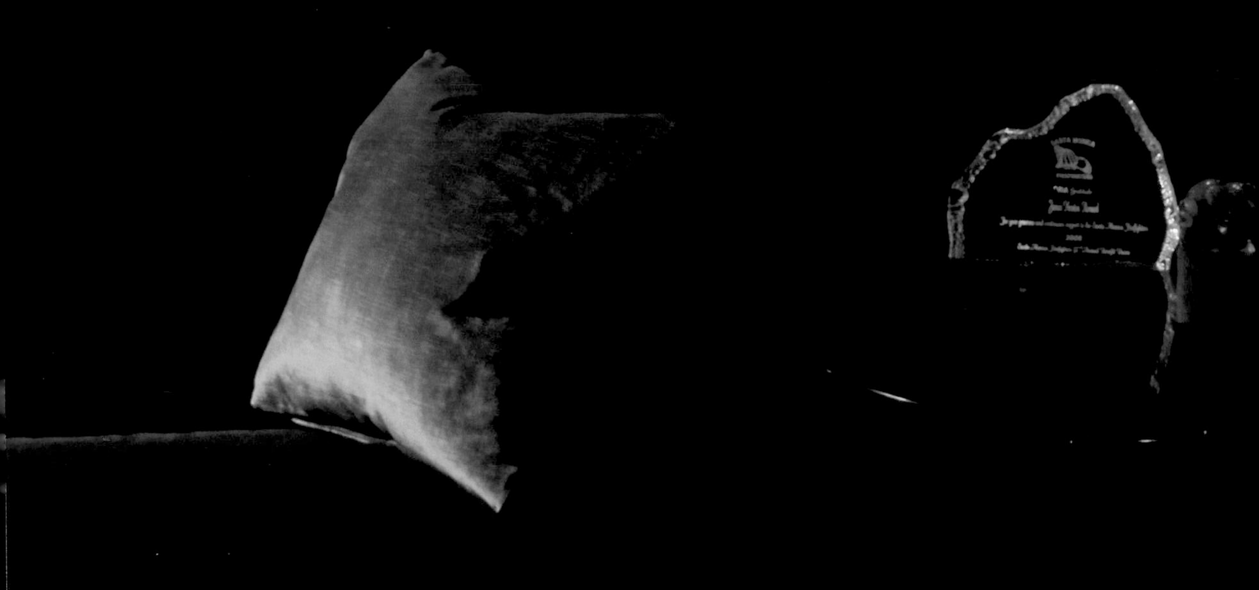

Pennsylvania 1999

Stanford 2009

Molino 2016

Edinburgh 2009

Palmer 2018

RCP 2007

Conversation

Hans Zimmer with Peter Grueneisen

PG Film composers sometimes work at the very start of the creative filmmaking process, even before any images exist. I think you said that about working with Chris Nolan. Unlike the actors and musicians, you may begin with just a concept or an idea. Are you drawn to that challenge?

HZ Actually, weirdly, it's the same as architecture. Somebody comes to you and says we're going to build a studio, we're going to build a house, and you become the architect and you're supposed to imagine it. Then you go out and get the laborers and the mechanics and put it all together. But we are basically the architect, the sonic architect, for this. Chris and I always found that it's better to work freely without having the dimensions dictated by something – by a cut, by an edit but to work freely within the imagination. Imagine as an architect you have unlimited resources and unlimited space, because you're building it all in your head.

PG Music reinforces, can even carry the emotional content of a film. Besides evoking a movie's essence, your music stands on its own. People listen to it apart from the films. Do you think of it as both part of the movie and a distinct work of art?

HZ Well, I think every piece of music has to be able to stand on its own two feet, aesthetically and practically. It can't – and that's my hubris, I suppose – I don't want it to just play a supporting role. I think every piece and every theme I write needs to be capable of having a life away from the movie. And that's why I did the tour where we wouldn't screen a single image. Because I wanted to find out if the music could really stand up by itself and be performed by musicians. You know, give it back to the musicians and look the audience in the eye, and do it in real time. It was important to not hide behind the screen for the rest of my life, or hide behind the story, but to see if my theory was true that things could stand up on their own. That was important.

PG You started out as a performer, then became the most prolific film composer of our time; now you have gone back to the stage for a series of highly acclaimed concerts around the world. It is apparent that you love working with the musicians and presenting your work live. What drew you to the idea to get out there again?

HZ Nothing drew me to the idea. I was beaten. I was whipped into going there! But my musicians ganged up on me; I could be very precise who it was. It was Johnny Marr; it was Pharrell Williams; it was Ann Marie Calhoun, who ganged up on me and said I had to stop hiding behind the screen. But I had terrible stage fright and so they said, "So what? Get used to it!" Every musician has to have stage fright. But you owe it to an audience; you owe it to go out there. Honestly, I still find it terrifying, but at the same time it's thrilling. You can't let fear stop you from doing things. The other thing I think is very important is that the operative word in music is play and, even if you're not a musician, to live a playful life. To play with other people is such a luxury; you should never lose that opportunity.

PG Music and architecture are often compared. One could draw parallels between film composers and architects, maybe more so than between the architect and the traditional music composer, the director, or the musician. Both invent original works but in collaboration with many others. Do you see any similarities?

HZ I think I have already answered that question! Absolutely. For instance, the way the Oscars think about collaboration, if I have twenty arrangers and orchestrators and programmers, etc. working on a piece of music, they can't be nominated; it has to be the architect of the original work. Even the Academy thinks of it as an architectural job. For instance, when James (Newton Howard) and I were doing *Batman*, or *Dark Knight* together, we had to convince the

Academy that we were co-architects of it. So it's very much like that, except the difference is that you architects are very disciplined. I see myself as more like a chef, and I go around and I go to the stores and see what's fresh. Carrots are fresh. Oh, tomatoes are fresh and potatoes are fresh. And then I spend a long time peeling them and chopping them up. And I know the guests are arriving at eight o'clock at night and at ten to eight I throw it all into a pot and hope that it's going to be delicious. I try to look for as many fresh things as possible and spend forever just chopping, chopping away.

PG Your composing room, designed by you long before we became involved with your buildings, is a very unique and iconic space. Does that physical environment impact the way you compose?

HZ It does. There's the acoustic part, which affects the way I write because one of the things I was after was completely neutral acoustics. You know, not too dead and not too live. And it's very easy to measure. If you can have a good conversation in the room, if the voice carries nicely, then it's a good room. Because what is very important as well is not just that the music I make in there sounds good; but that the conversations we have amongst ourselves, amongst musicians and directors, become effortless. And that the room invites you to have ideas and collaborations and that people want to have creative ideas and feel safe to say anything they want to say and to play any note they want to play. The architecture and the acoustics are very important in how it seduces you into having ideas. People always thought I was a little crazy when I built the room, but I think it actually turned out quite the opposite – that people come there because they know you can have the freedom to have ideas, the freedom to experiment. Ron Howard keeps calling it the laboratory, and he keeps saying don't shut the laboratory doors too soon. He likes the idea that people are free to be creative, to make up ideas and speak about them, to just pick up an instrument and play.

PG You have described your studio as resembling a 19th century Viennese bordello. It is very rich and layered, very detailed. Yet you have encouraged us to pursue a very different, more modernist and minimalist approach with the projects we have done together. Do you see that as similar to how different movies demand their own musical aesthetic?

HZ: No, not really. Well, of course, but that's not really the point. I just think it's really interesting to be surrounded by different aesthetics, by many different voices and many different cultures. I like the idea that on the doors, because we have people from so many different cultures, it doesn't say Heitor Pereira, for example, but it has a Brazilian flag. I like that people from all nations and upbringing are bringing a bit of culture with them and into this pot of music and storytelling. And the same goes for the aesthetic. Something can be incredibly modern and streamlined. If I could, I would have another room which would be my Kandinsky Bauhaus room because both things appeal to me.
I remember, for instance, when you did Atli's (Örvarsson) room. I knew the walls weren't going to be right for him because he was Icelandic, and I knew he needed to have an endless horizon. I don't know if you remember, but I think he got his wife to repaint the fabric so it became like looking out across Iceland with an endless horizon because that would be where he would feel comfortable. Where I feel comfortable, I suppose, is at the edge of German Jugendstil tradition.

PG Most architects operate within a confined formal language. You created a very eclectic musical body of work, from the delicate melodies in *Driving Miss Daisy* and *Gladiator*, the World Music in *The Lion King* to the organ of *Interstellar* and the pounding rhythms of *Dunkirk*. It must be fun to explore in that way!

HZ Absolutely! But I think that's because... Look, I grew up in a Bauhaus, a true Bauhaus. What would there be without Peter Behrens? He was the teacher for all those other guys, Frank Lloyd Wright or any of those people, but I grew up in that environment, listening to classical music and to music from all over the world. So my upbringing was multicultural and multistylistic. In the words of Duke Ellington, there are only two types of music, good music or bad music. But I will write my baroque, psychedelic, country western album one of these days, with a lot of electronica in it.

PG Some composers (and architects) think of themselves as solitary heroes. But we live in an age of collaboration, and your model of cooperation stands out in its commitment to the variety and diversity of our time. It reminds me of the Renaissance workshops of Leonardo da Vinci and others, in their dedication to create but also to be a mentors.

HZ The question is basically who is the mentor and who is the teacher, because the roles change constantly. Some young kid will come up with some crazy

fabulous idea, and you are listening to them and they are listening to you, and that's the thing. It's a constant exchange of ideas. When you come from a band, you can take the boy out of the band but you can't take the band out of the boy. Don't architects work like this as well? I remember going over to Frank Gehry's place, and there are people doing experiments and trying new materials and loads of people just trying things out or seeing what works.
But you know, at the same time you're coming back to the question of aesthetics. At the end of the day it doesn't matter how many people are working with me, it's still me, without a shadow of a doubt. Actually, here is a good example: If you take the movies I did with Ridley Scott, they say as much about Ridley Scott as they do about me. They're stylistically incredibly different. *Gladiator, Thelma and Louise, Black Rain, Black Hawk Down, Matchstick Men*, I'm sure I'm forgetting a few, but it doesn't matter. *Gladiator* and *Thelma and Louise* couldn't sound more different from each other, but they are still unmistakably me, and unmistakably Ridley Scott. Just because we work in many, many different styles doesn't mean we lose our identity. Or we can work with a lot of people in our team, in our bands, you can still tell, oh, hang on, there was an architect, and his style was sort of unmistakable.

PG: Given the title of this book, I have to ask: You have created a memorable score for *Inception* as part of your collaboration with director Christopher Nolan. Dreams are at the core of that movie, with their complete disassociation of space and time and their divorce from reality. Yet they remain intimately intertwined with the real lives, to the point where it is difficult to recognize the difference. Did that movie resonate with you as a metaphor for the making of films and music?

HZ It wasn't so much about that. Well, it was, yes, but the process of making music is very similar. It's like you have a room full of people who don't say a word to each other, but there's a moment of shared dreaming. And I think the same thing happens in the cinema with the audience. You know, they are all having an autonomous separate experience alone together, if that makes any sense. And for me, we are all alone in this together; that is what I find really interesting.

Hans Zimmer is a preeminent film composer and musician. He works out of his Remote Control Productions studios when he is not touring with his band and orchestra.

Hans Zimmer's laboratory

Remote Control
Santa Monica, California

Remote Control Productions occupies a complex of several buildings located within a Santa Monica city block. Built during different time periods and with varying sizes, shapes, and materials, they form a varied assembly, straddling two different light industrial and commercial city zones. The site is owned and occupied by Hans Zimmer, an acclaimed film composer, with some of the best known contemporary movie scores to his credit.

The urban campus is inhabited by a group of collaborating composers, musicians, and sound engineers, as well as technical and administrative support staff. The unusual enterprise offers unique opportunities for young and talented composers to engage in artistic collaborations, and is unmatched within the industry in its composition and creative output.

The multiple projects, designed and constructed over more than a decade, create a unified identity for the company and its artists while reinforcing the strong social and artistic networking aspects within the group of occupants.

The overall objective is to develop of a cohesive campus and to create a sustainable and environmentally sensitive neighborhood. Preserving the varying scales and characters of the different buildings, typical for the eclectic neighborhood, is part of the goal. Much like the ongoing collaborations between the artists, the design fosters both individuality and the common ground among the buildings.

Individual properties have been improved or rebuilt to develop modern and sensibly scaled creative work environments, while production continued in other areas of the campus. The program includes music composition and recording suites, technical support space and administrative and lounge areas.

Typical building materials reflect the industrial heritage of the area, but their detailing and applications hint at the building's contemporary use. Main elements used throughout are photovoltaic panels, galvanized metal cladding, smooth gray plaster, perforated metal screens, and fritted glass panels. Some of the characteristic red brick remains either fully exposed or shown behind screens.

A crucial part of the strategy for a sustainable project is the protection and reuse of most of the existing building substance. Remodeling the old buildings and improving them in a sensitive and appropriately scaled manner, rather than rebuilding them from scratch, saves considerable materials and energy.

The creation of music and sound for films is a very energy-intensive process. A facility operating at the highest technical level consumes enormous amounts of electricity. The updates to the complex include the implementation of a comprehensive solar energy strategy, aiming to be exemplary for the film and music production industry. The goal is to generate a large portion of the power requirements through solar energy and to use the requisite building elements to create a recognizable and architecturally sensitive environment.

The alley between the buildings, which already serves as an informal outdoor meeting space, will eventually be improved with parking canopies. Covered with glass and integrated photovoltaic cells, the roofs will provide shade, while letting filtered sunlight through and generating electrical power.

One eventually abandoned project included a large film scoring stage for orchestral recording. Inserted into an existing brick building, the stage was to house more than sixty musicians and choral singers. The roof was to be covered entirely with solar panels, which extend to shade an outdoor patio on the former roof level. The project may now be realized on a different site.

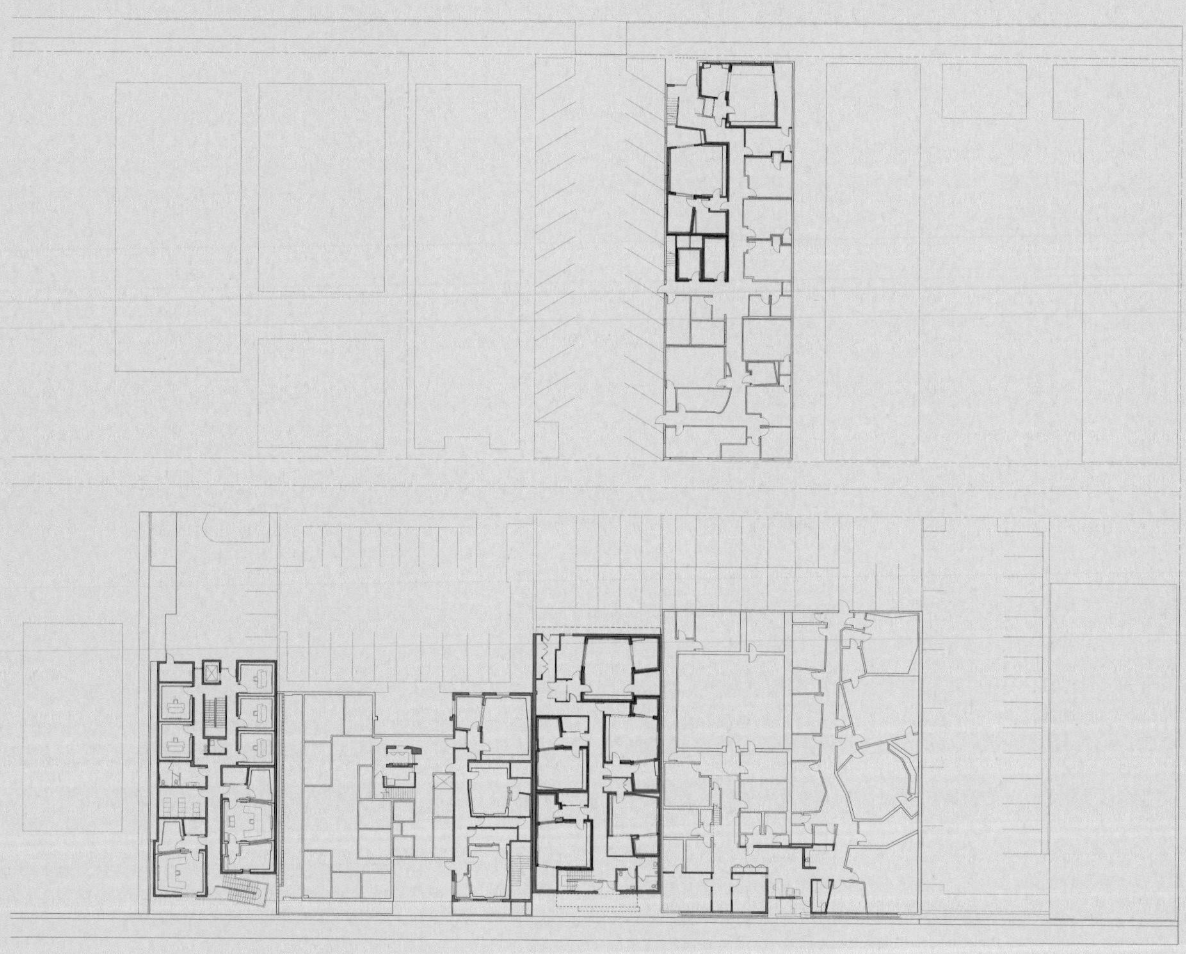

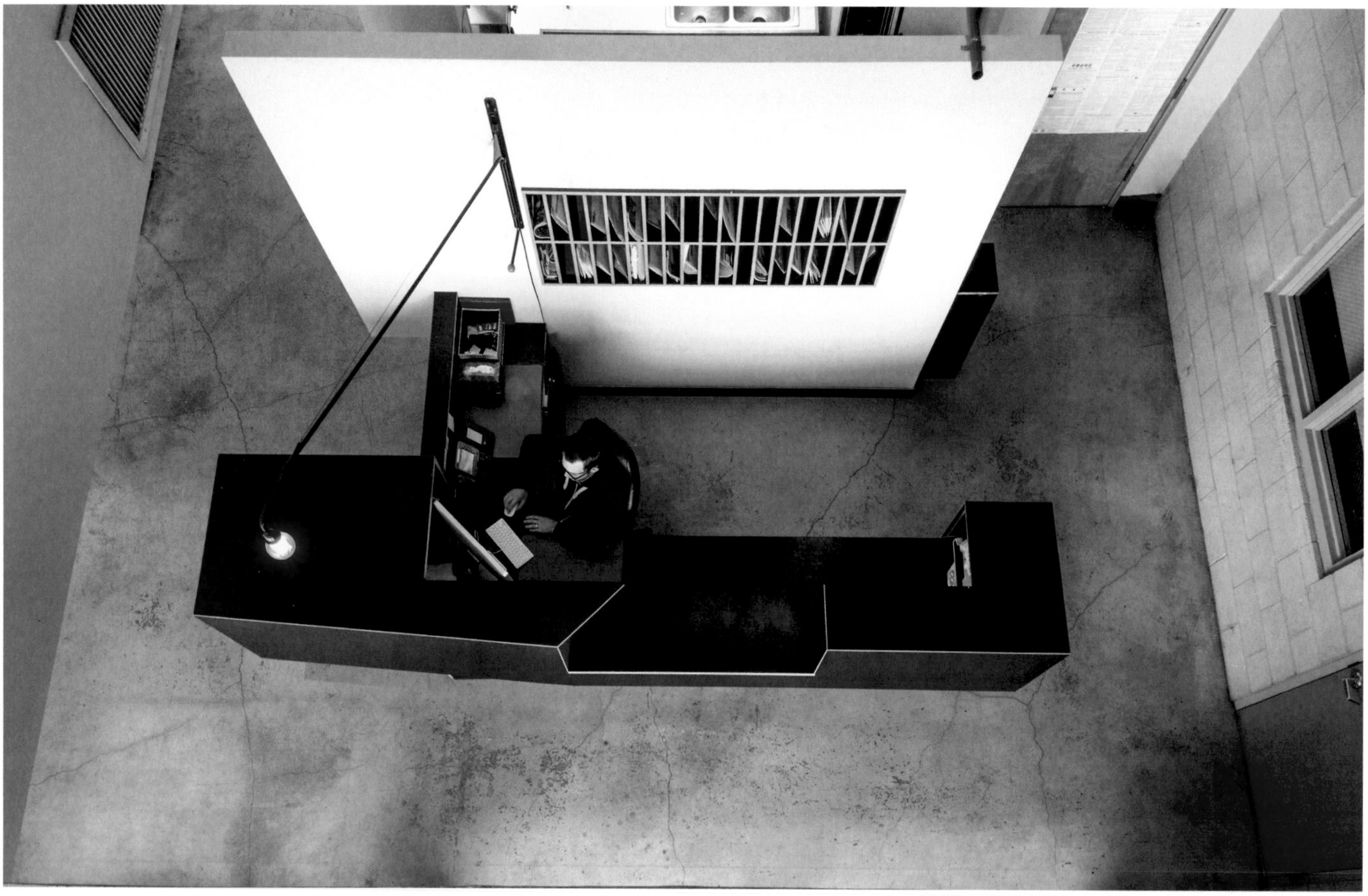

Proposed scoring stage project and solar canopy in shared alley

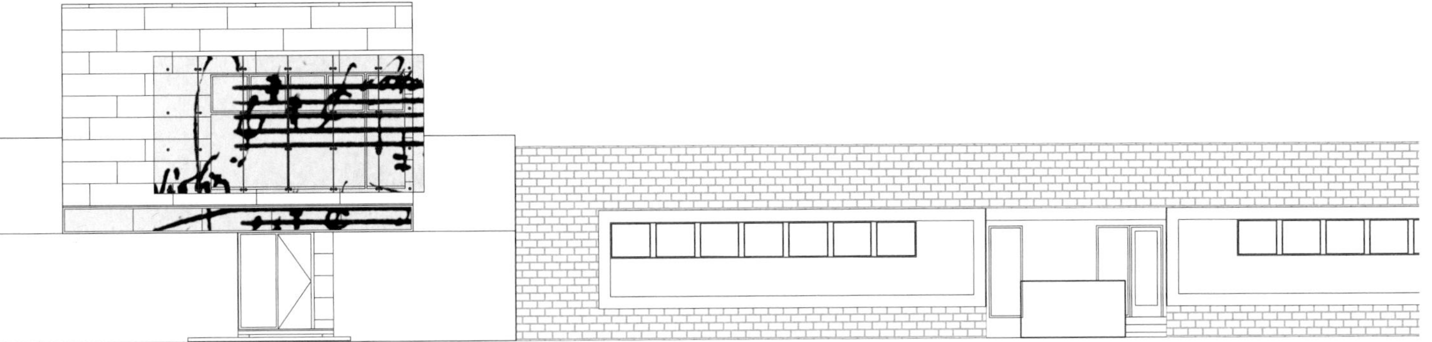

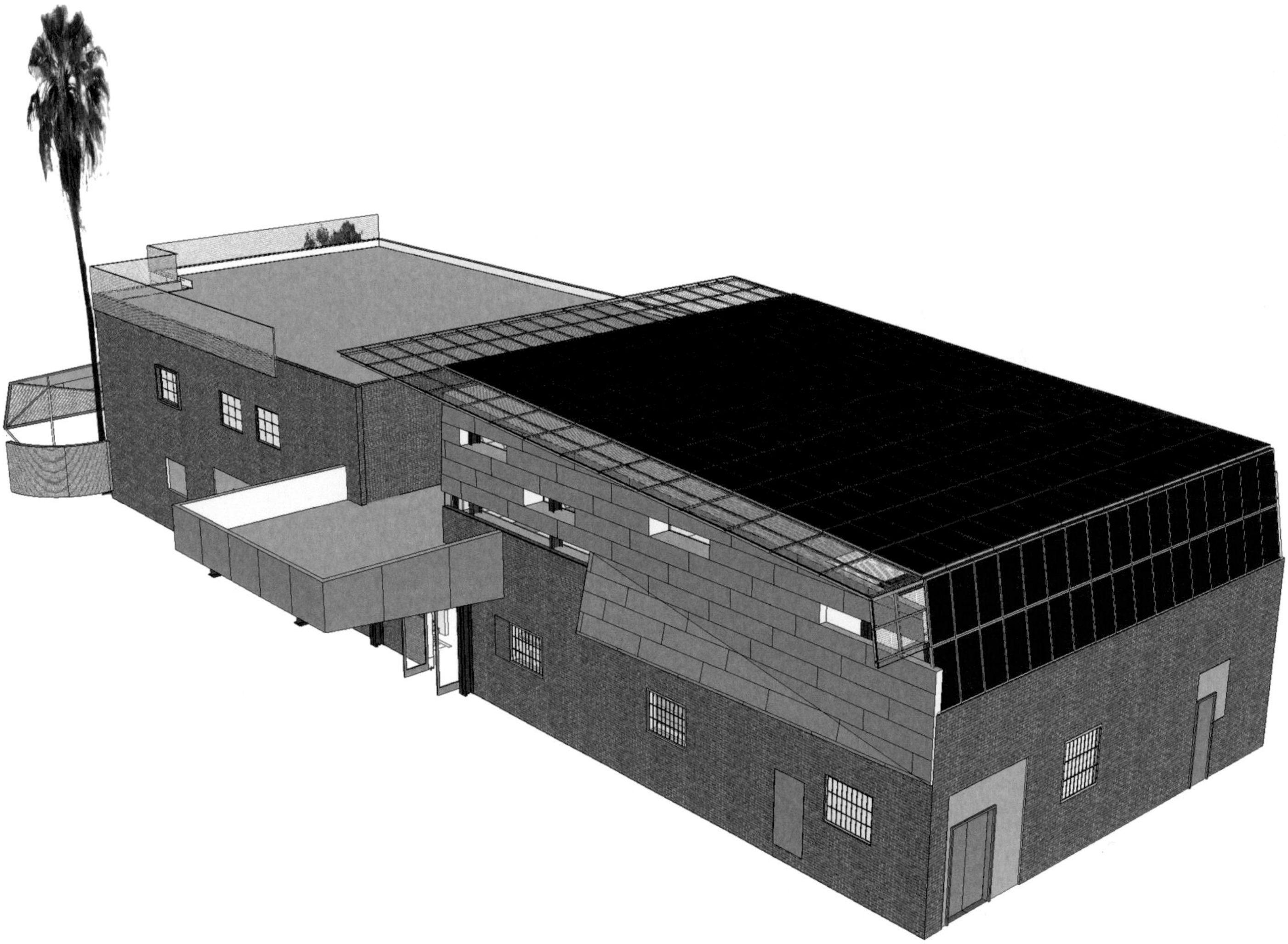

Proposed Scoring Stage

Remote Control 1537

Santa Monica, California

The project, which was completed in 2009, includes the transformation of an existing commercial office building and warehouse into a music composition facility. To allow the parking spaces to remain at the existing number, the city required an unaltered footprint with minimally changed exterior walls. Both floors were rebuilt taller but within the same layout as before, retaining the ground floor exterior walls. Sculpted concrete blocks making up the rear wall are a reminder of the original building. Not much else remains of the previous structure; a portion of the roof, initially meant to be retained, was discovered to have fire damage and had to be removed.

Although the footprint could not be changed, the three-dimensional massing, the fenestration, and the materiality of the detailing turned an unremarkable building into a more sophisticated composition.

Five studio suites with writing rooms, recording booths, assistants' studios, and equipment rooms were developed with their individual composer tenants on the ground floor. Four more standardized music edit rooms were placed on the smaller upper level, adjacent to a shared lounge with an outdoor roof deck.

The large skylight over the main hallway is at the center of the design and offers relief from the intense process of creating music for films and television in dark and hermetically sealed studios. The west-facing lounge on the second floor is tempered by large glass panels that serve as a passive solar shading screen and provide privacy. Its fritted pattern of a partial handwritten score by W. A. Mozart was enlarged nearly to the point of abstraction, when viewed from the adjacent street below. It continues on the glass below and may eventually be extended across several adjacent buildings in future expansions.

Photovoltaic panels on the roofs are used to offset the energy-intensive music production process. The building design was conceived as the starting point for further developments on the eclectic site and to set a precedent within the overall master plan.

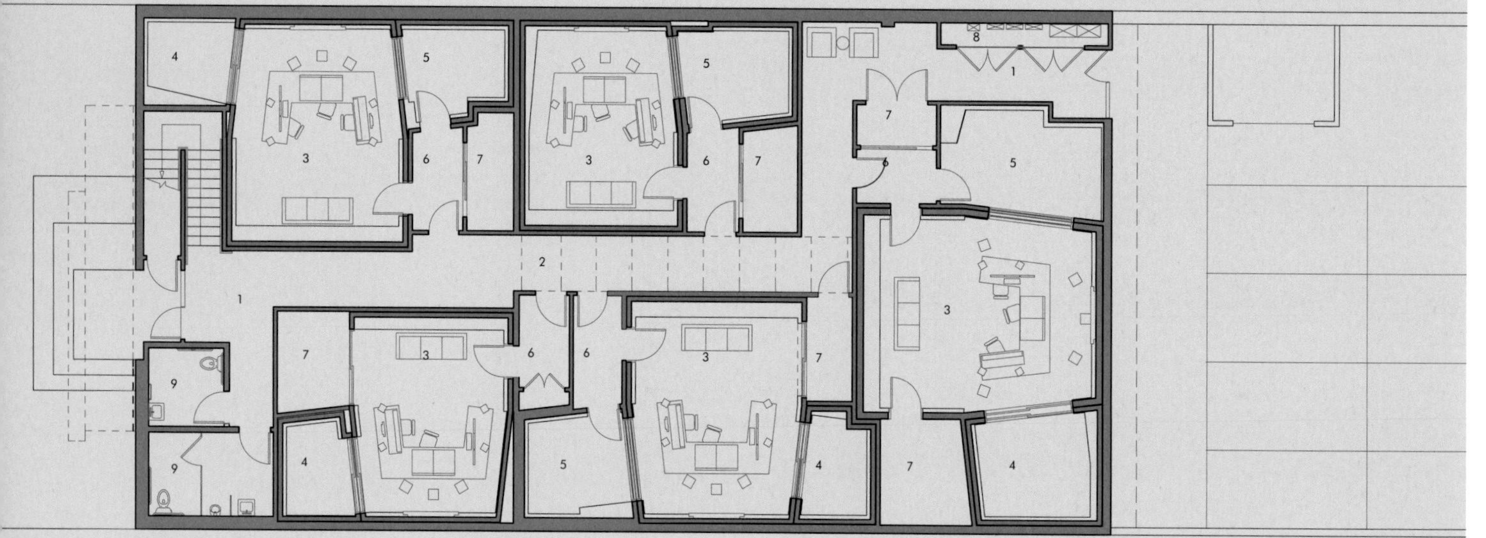

GROUND FLOOR PLAN

1	Entry	6	Vestibule
2	Hallway	7	Equipment Room
3	Music Composition Room	8	Electrical Room
4	Iso Booth	9	Restroom
5	Iso Booth/Assistant		

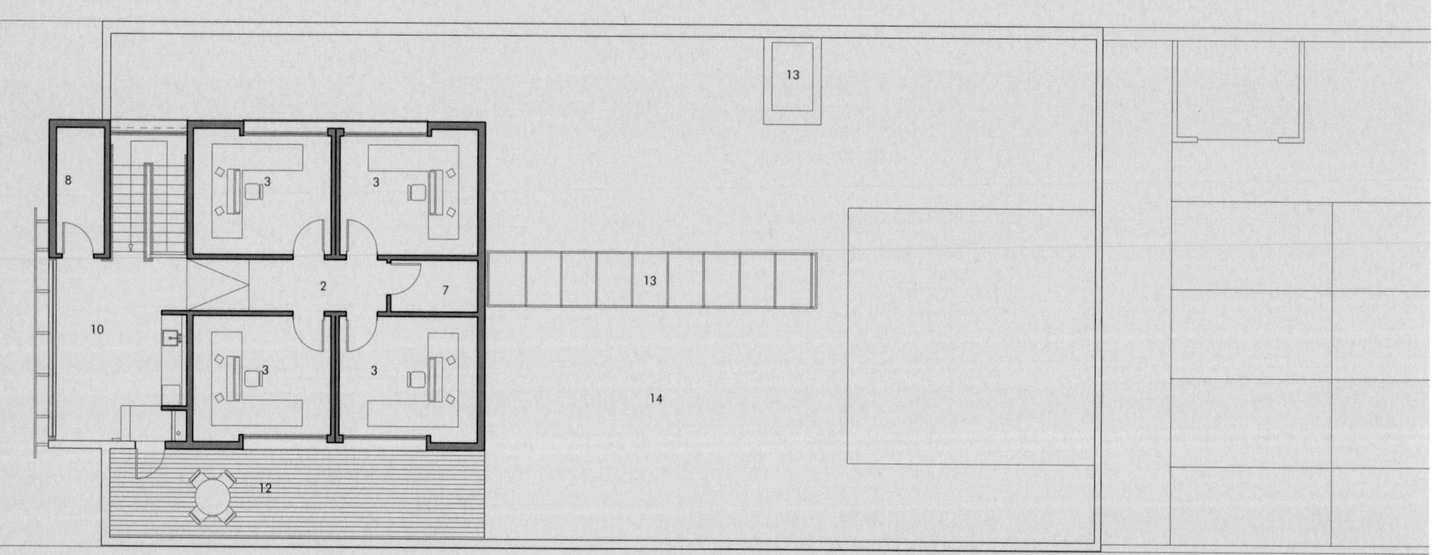

SECOND FLOOR PLAN

2	Hallway	10	Lounge
3	Music Composition Room	12	Patio
7	Equipment Room	13	Skylight
8	Electrical Room	14	Proof

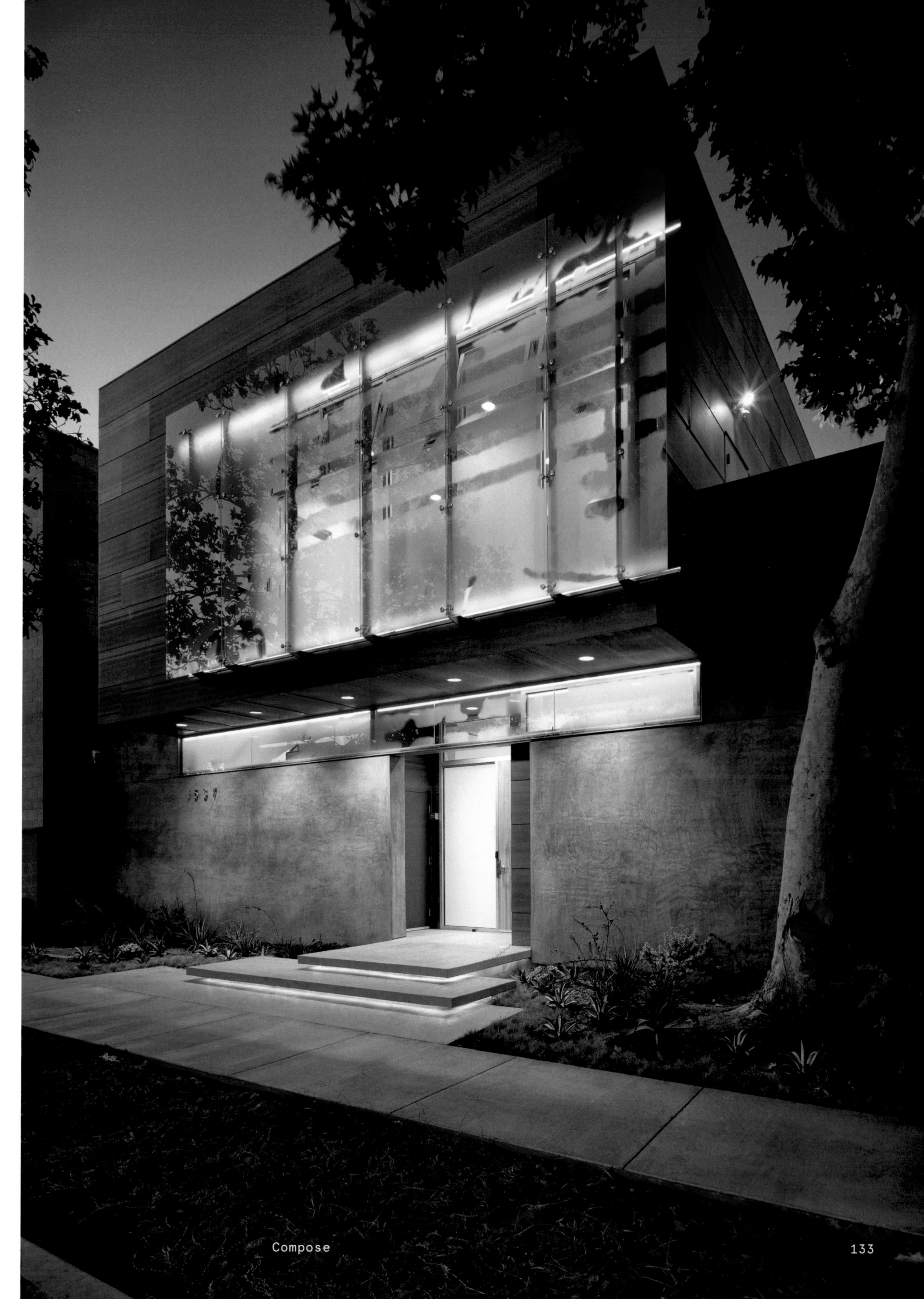

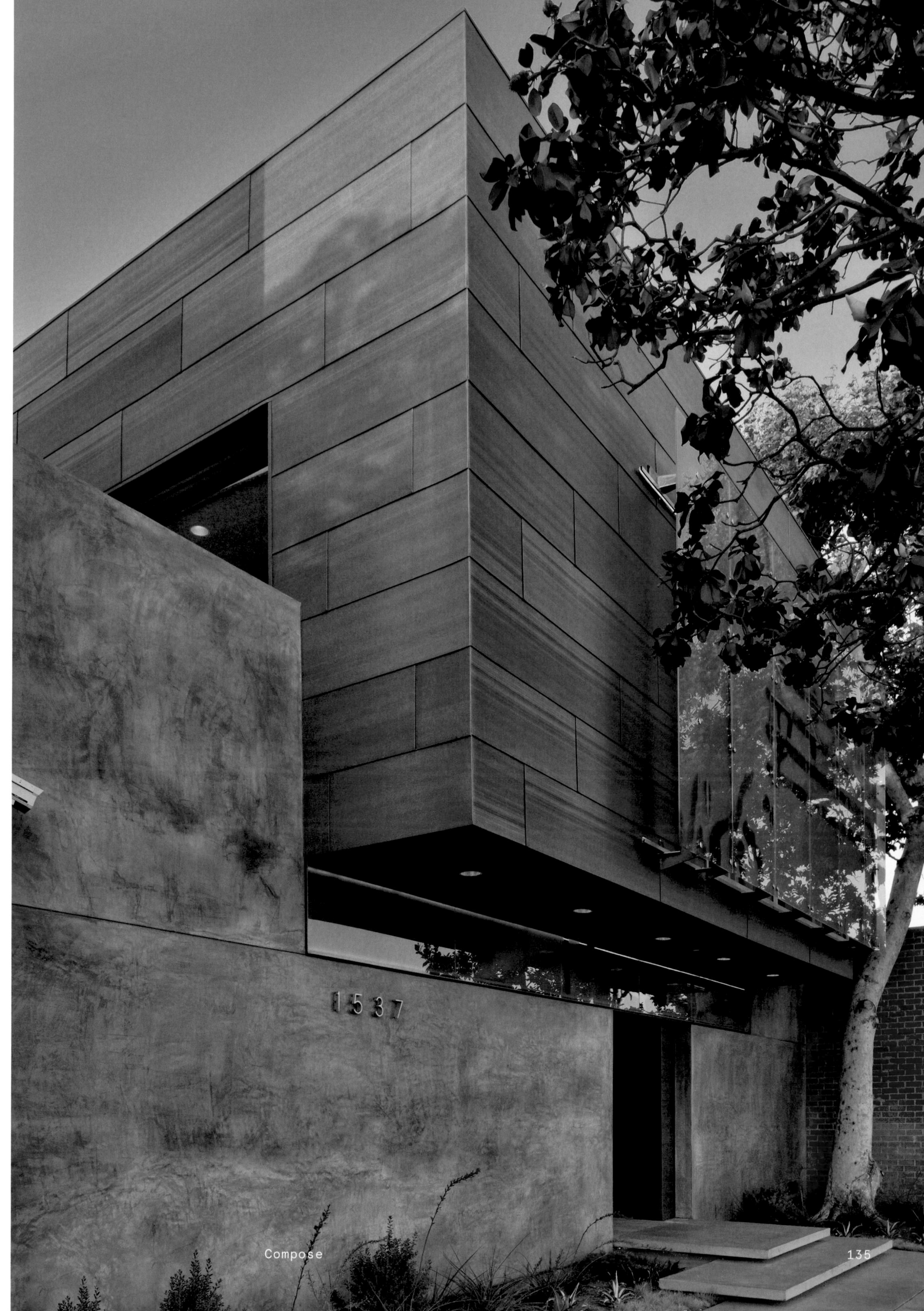
1537

1537

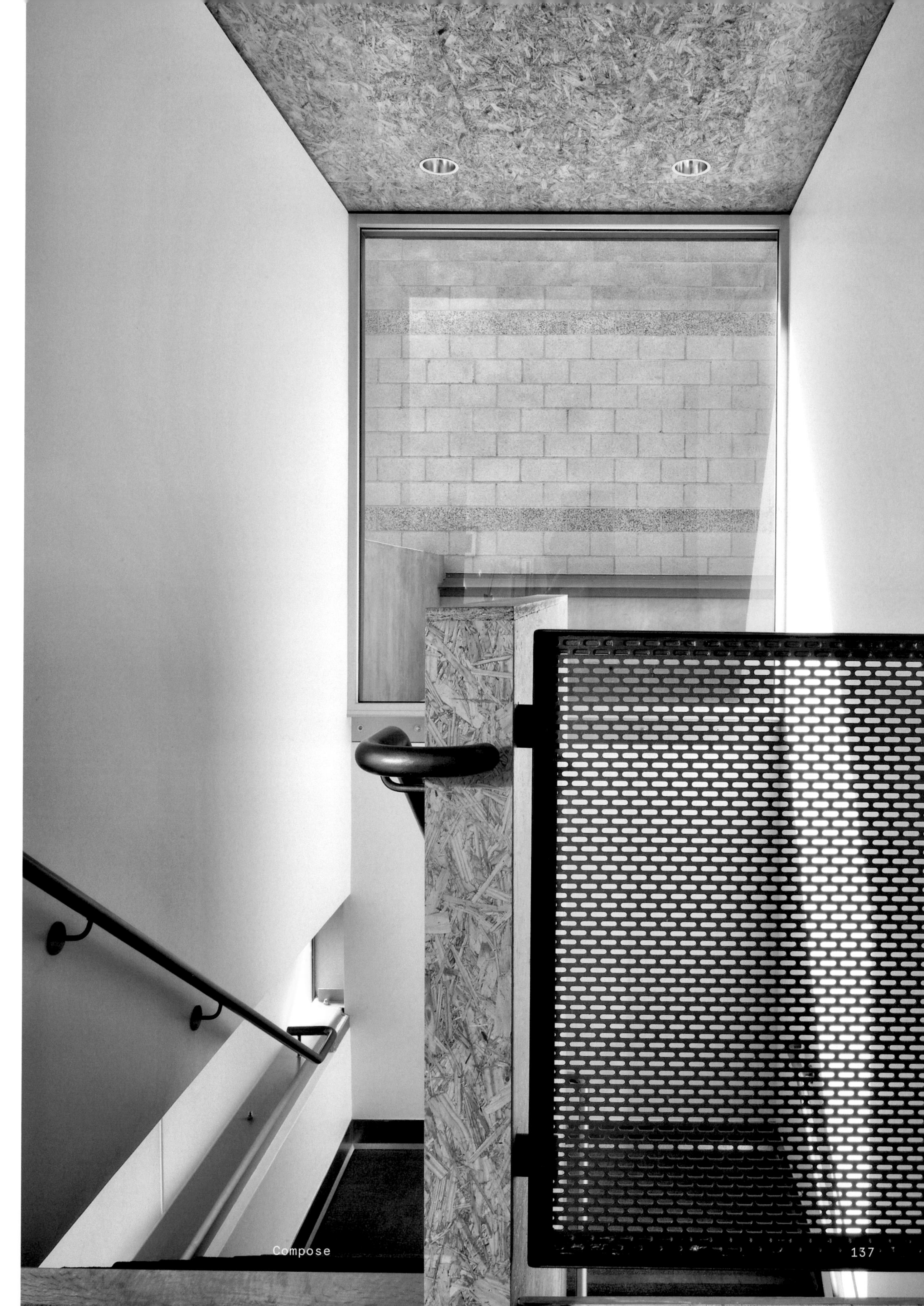

1537

Remote Control 1523
Santa Monica, California

The second ground-up structure on the expanding campus was completed in 2014 on a previously empty brownfield lot as part of an ongoing master plan. The limited size of the lot and the city's parking requirements required a remote parking lot on a second parcel. A few years before, a design was completed to replace a dilapidated building further to the south, but the parking lot now takes up that space. Due to the construction of the Metro light rail line along the southern edge of the campus, the locations of the building and the parking were reversed from the original master plan, to increase the distance of the recording studios from the train tracks.

The building includes two larger individual composition and recording suites on the ground level, but most of it is used for sixteen smaller audio production studios. Like all buildings on the campus, this one also includes a small lounge to complement the main kitchen, dining, and community area across the alley. The enclosed nature of the workspaces demands some relief, provided in the form of spaces with strong connections to daylight and the surrounding environment. A strategy of offering a variety of naturally lit and exterior spaces was pursued, resulting in an almost entirely skylit second floor, a long cantilevered balcony in the back, and the lounge overlooking the street.

In front of the lounge, a moveable portion of the screens wrapping around the building allows for either increased views to the trees and the street or for more sun protection from the west. The aluminum panels offer shading and privacy, but they are also used for guardrails and separation panels inside and outside the building. They are perforated with a pattern derived from vintage synthesizer modules, a tool used by many of the resident composers. Continuing the musical theme introduced in the previous building with the glass Mozart score, the abstracted patterns allude to a different aspect of the work being done inside.

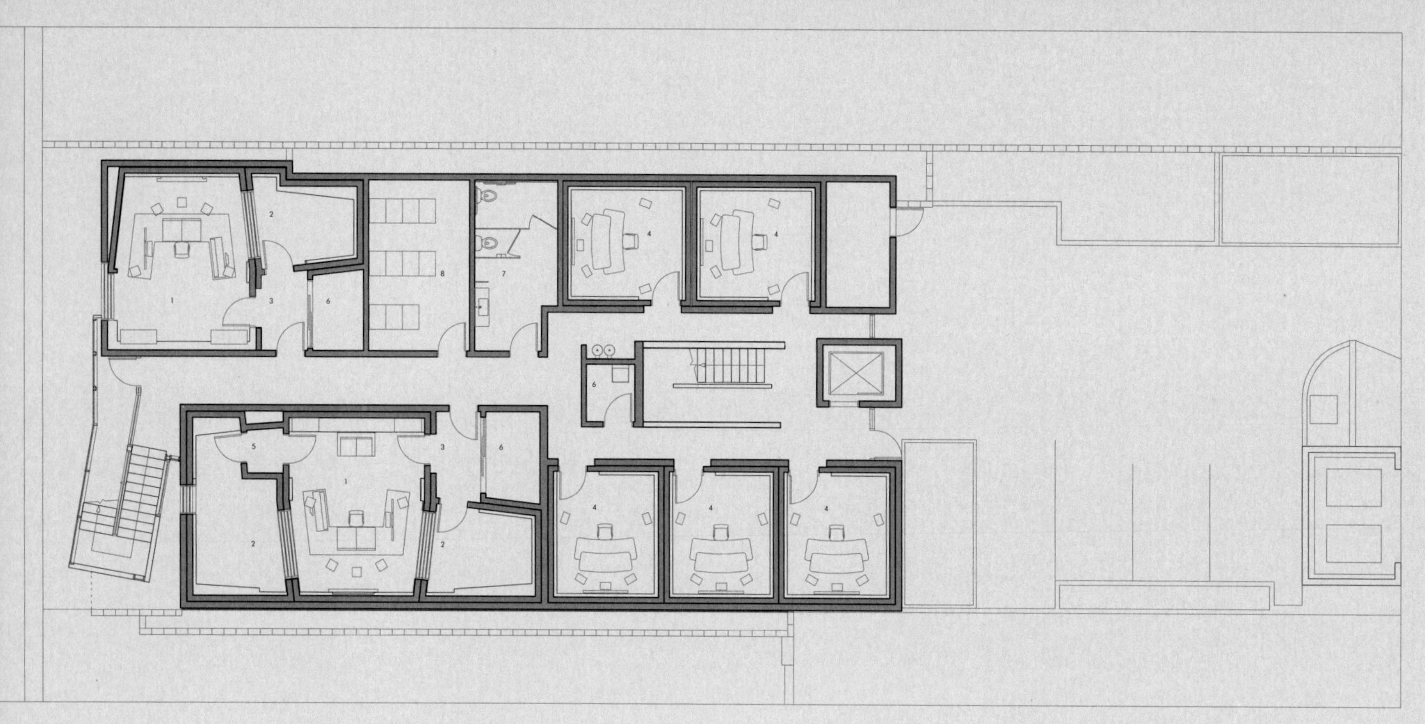

GROUND FLOOR PLAN

1	Mix Room	5	Sound Lock
2	Isolation Room	6	Closet
3	Vestibule	7	Bathroom
4	Music Room	8	Machine Room

SECOND FLOOR PLAN

1	Storage	4	Women's Bathroom
2	Lounge	5	Balcony
3	Music Room	6	Equipment Room

1523

1523

1523

1523

EXIT
EXIT
EXIT

1523

Elbo
Glendale, California

This film music composition and production facility occupies a former industrial warehouse near the Metro station in Glendale, just north of Los Angeles. While close to ideal in most other aspects, the chosen location demanded extensive soundproofing and vibration controls, due to the trains' piercing horns and their movement on the iron tracks. But after a long search for the perfect location, this was a problem that could be overcome.

The project's owner, a renowned film composer, asked for a recording space that could accommodate up to 30 musicians for orchestral scoring, supplemented by two isolation booths for drums and piano. The adjacent control room would also serve as a mix room. Besides these more public spaces, a personal writing and composition room with a recording booth was included for his own composition work.

A second music composition suite and several smaller production rooms complete the build-out, while another section of the studio footprint was initially set aside for future expansion. As a fitting neighbor and constant reminder of film music's storied history, the remaining half of the building houses an archive of classic film scores.

A few years after the initial completion of the project, the leftover studio space was built out as well. The occupant of the second original suite, having found extraordinary success with his own musical work, decided to claim it for his work and to give it its own distinctive vibe.

The entrance courtyard, lounge and kitchen area were designed in collaboration with Barbara Bestor, who had previously completed a residential project for the owner and had initially brought the team together.

The main tracking room and its piano booth are treated with distinctively perforated maple panels and a diffusive gypsum bubble pattern. The floating concrete slabs are polished and the remaining wall and ceiling areas are treated with absorptive fabric surfaces. A large drape can be pulled across the back wall to adjust the room's acoustic properties and area rugs dampen the floor's reflectivity.

In contrast to the muted natural colors used for the initial build-out, the later expansion features bold green fabrics, a skylight and mirrored ceilings. Its main technical feature is not primarily sound related but consists of a ping-pong table that can be raised out of the recording space's oak floor. A secondary floor then rises up and protects the depression, left behind by the floor turned playing surface. Utilizing this unique opportunity, the large cavity necessary for the mechanism was then turned into an echo chamber equipped with subterranean microphone and speaker connections. With these elements and a large roll-down projection screen, the space can be used as a creative laboratory in multiple ways, as a recording studio, a living room and a playroom.

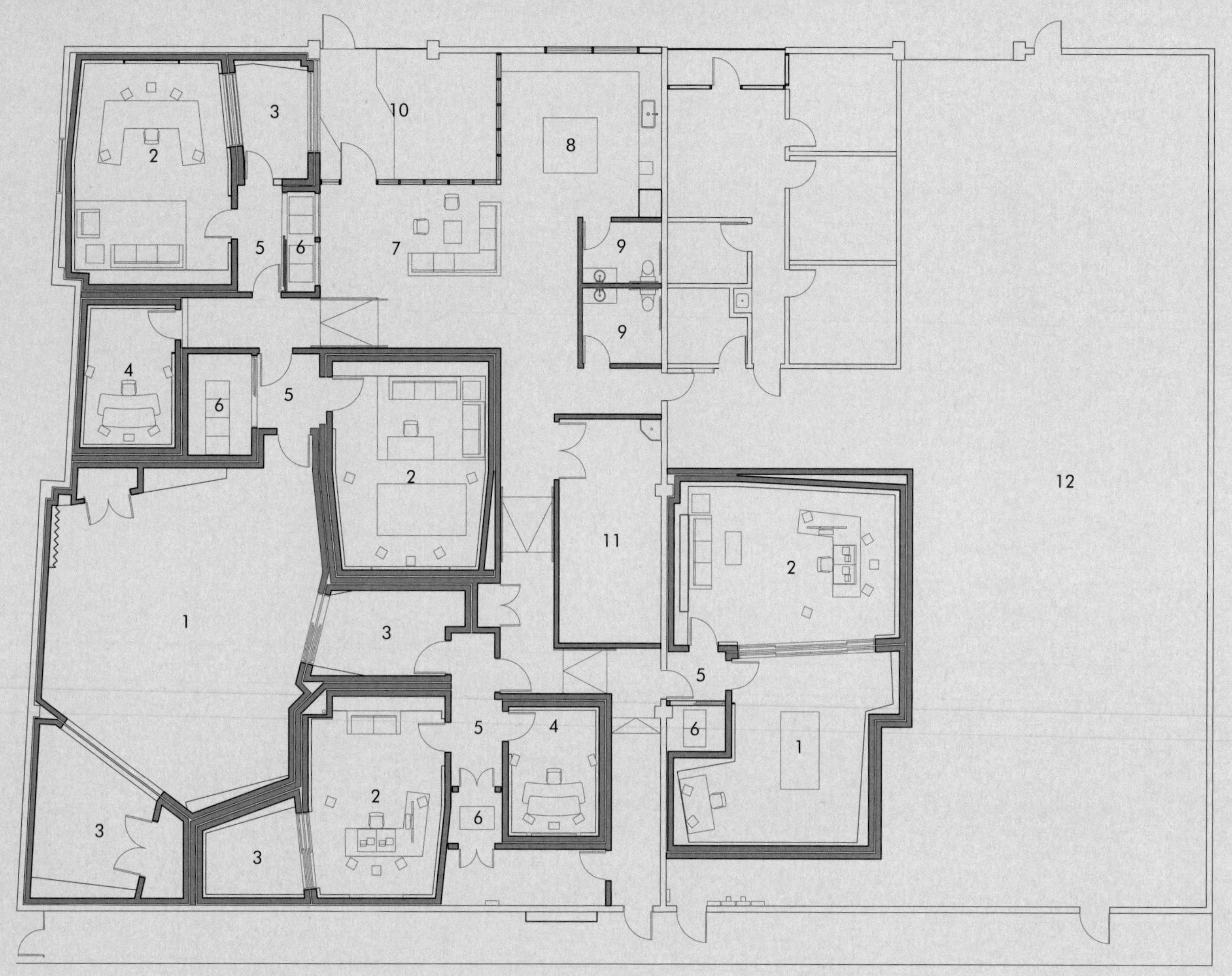

FLOOR PLAN

1 Tracking Room
2 Control/Mix Room
3 Isolation Booth
4 Production Room
5 Sound Lock
6 Equipment Room
7 Lounge
8 Kitchen
9 Bathroom
10 Atrium
11 Storage
12 Tenant Space

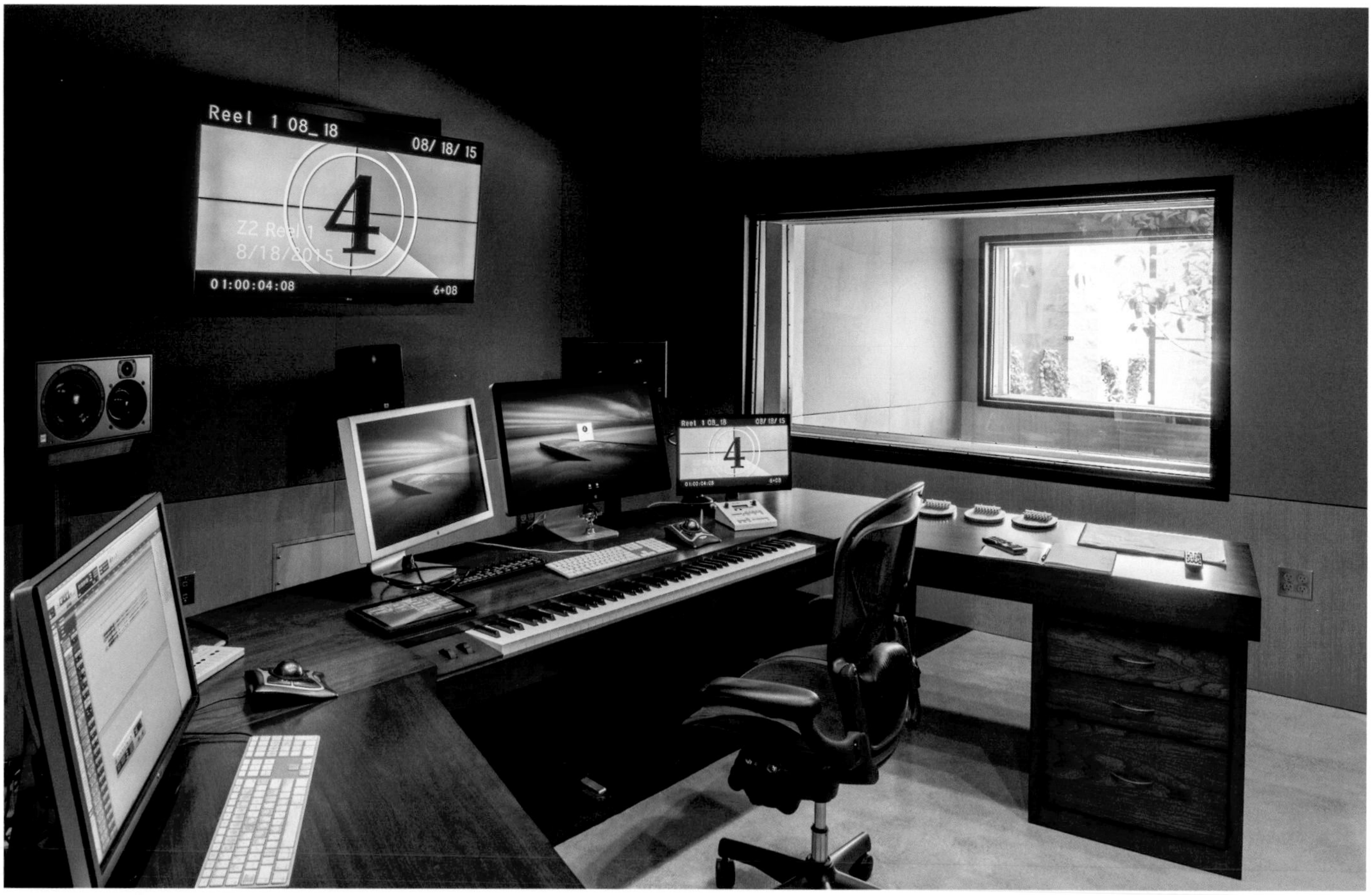
Reel 1 08_18
08/ 18/ 15
4
Z2 Reel 1
8/18/2015
01:00:04:08
6+08

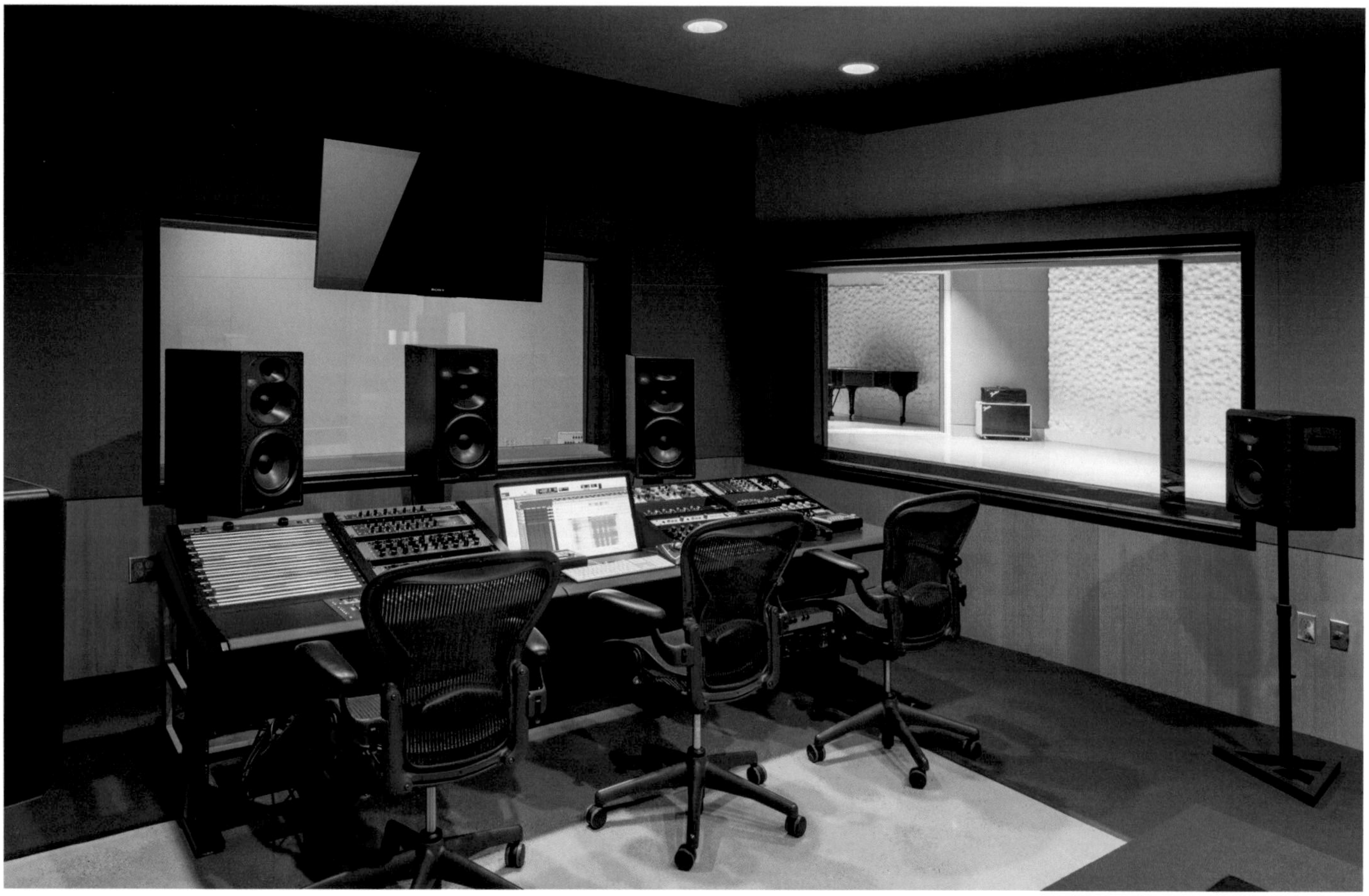

Following pages:
The expansion of the studio by another composer is distinctly different from the first phase. The ping pong table rises out of the floor or disappears completely.

Momentum
Santa Monica, California

The 3,000 square-foot space is located in a small business park in Santa Monica's creative core. Although it had earlier been built out by a previous tenant as a postproduction facility, the existing studios had to be removed and completely rebuilt to the new much stricter requirements of the composers taking it over.

Two primary composing rooms are complemented by workspaces for assistants, a lobby and a conference room with a kitchenette. While the smaller of the studios features an adjacent recording space, the larger one is equipped for the presentation of ongoing work and final scores to directors and executives. A row of comfortable theater seats on a raised platform in the rear of the room accommodates visitors for that purpose. It is finished in richer and darker colors, while the smaller control and writing room and its recording booth are themed with lighter woods.

The entrance lobby benefits from existing skylights and north-facing windows. The conference room inserted into the space is kept as transparent as possible with frameless glass partitions and sliding glass doors for spatial continuity. While relatively modest in its dimensions, the openness of the front and the denser concentration of rooms towards the back help give the facility the appearance of a larger space.

After several years of collaboration at Momentum, the owners dissolved their partnership and decided to give up the leased space in Santa Monica. The senior partner, a highly renowned composer and orchestral arranger, owned a large, level property with a rarely used tennis court. To consolidate and reduce both his commute and overhead, he decided to create a new studio for himself closer to home.

While the distant location and the rising costs in Santa Monica were the reasons to relocate, the functionality and the feel of the previous facility were deemed a success and served as the model for the new design. After some design attempts to integrate the new studio by adding on to an existing accessory studio building, a free-standing ground-up structure was determined to offer more advantages.

The scheme is kept as low as possible to fit into the residential neighborhood and the fiber cement facade alludes to the vertical wood board and batten cladding of the existing house. A basic square floor plan contributes to an economical design enhanced by the internal spatial composition and careful detailing. The studio structure occupies about half of the former tennis court; the remaining half is used for parking.

The studios are reminiscent of the previous facility and the common areas also feature tall ceilings and an exposed wooden roof structure. The main difference from the old studios is the new location in a suburban garden, away from traffic and other distractions.

FLOOR PLAN
Momentum Santa Monica

1 Composition Room
2 Studio
3 Production Room
4 Office/Tech Shop
5 Conference Room
6 Lobby/Lounge
7 Restroom
8 Vestibule
9 Equipment Room
10 Electrical/Storage

FLOOR PLAN
Momentum Hatteras

1 Existing House
2 Existing Studio
3 Composition Room
4 Studio
5 Office/Production
6 Lobby/Lounge
7 Equipment Room
8 Restroom
9 Pool
10 Parking

MOMENTUM

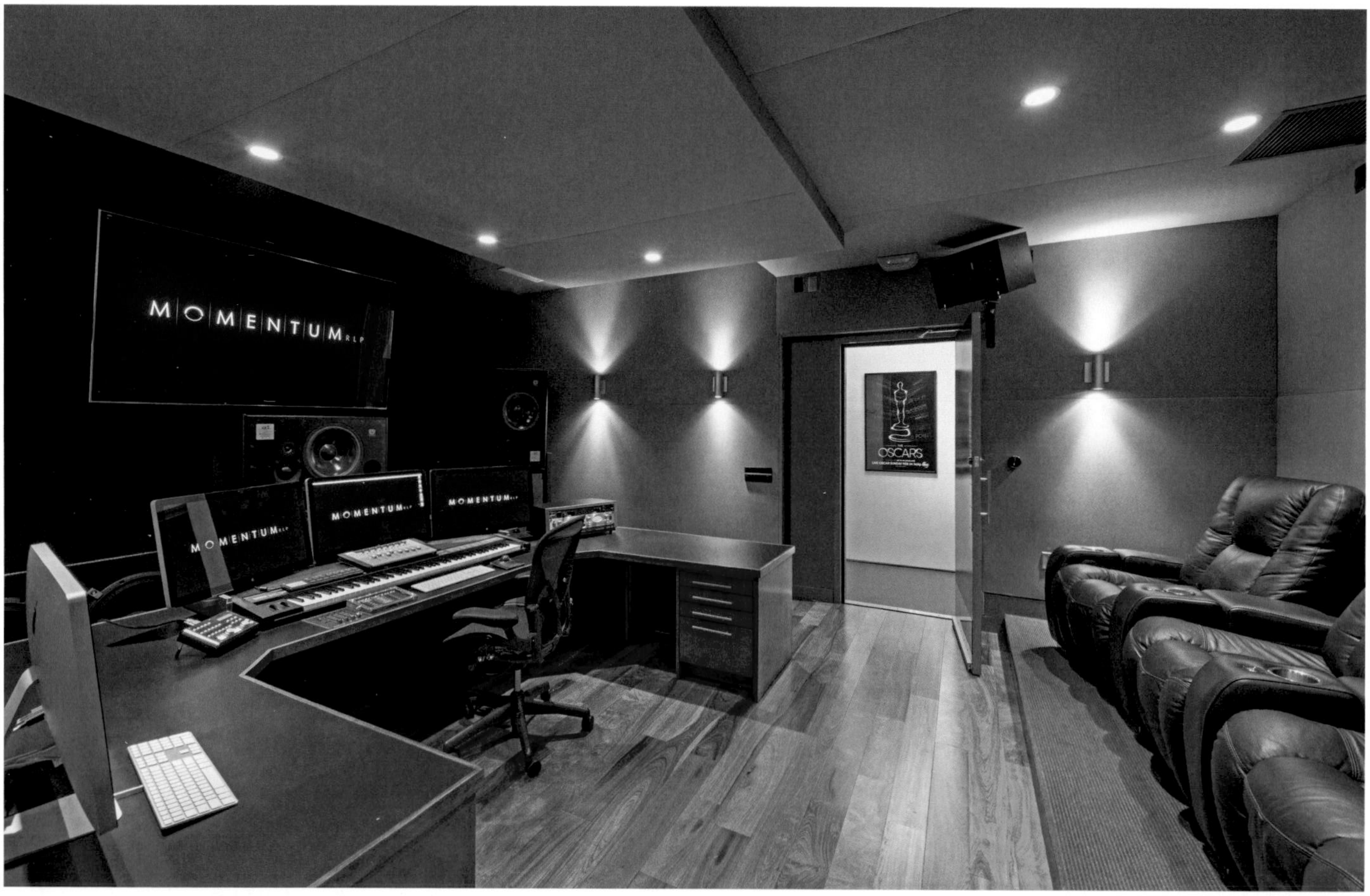
MOMENTUM
OSCARS

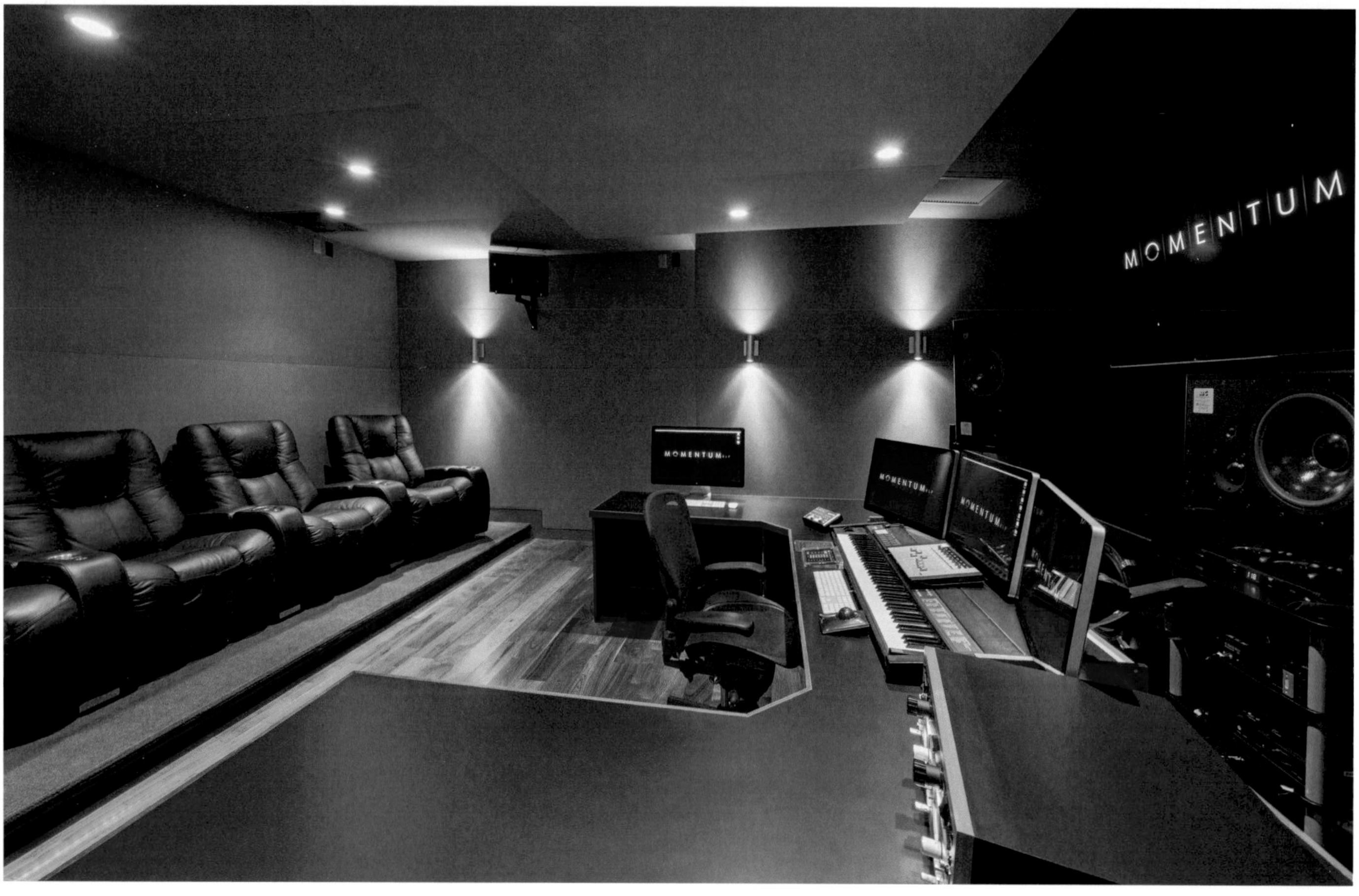
MOMENTUM

MOMENTUM

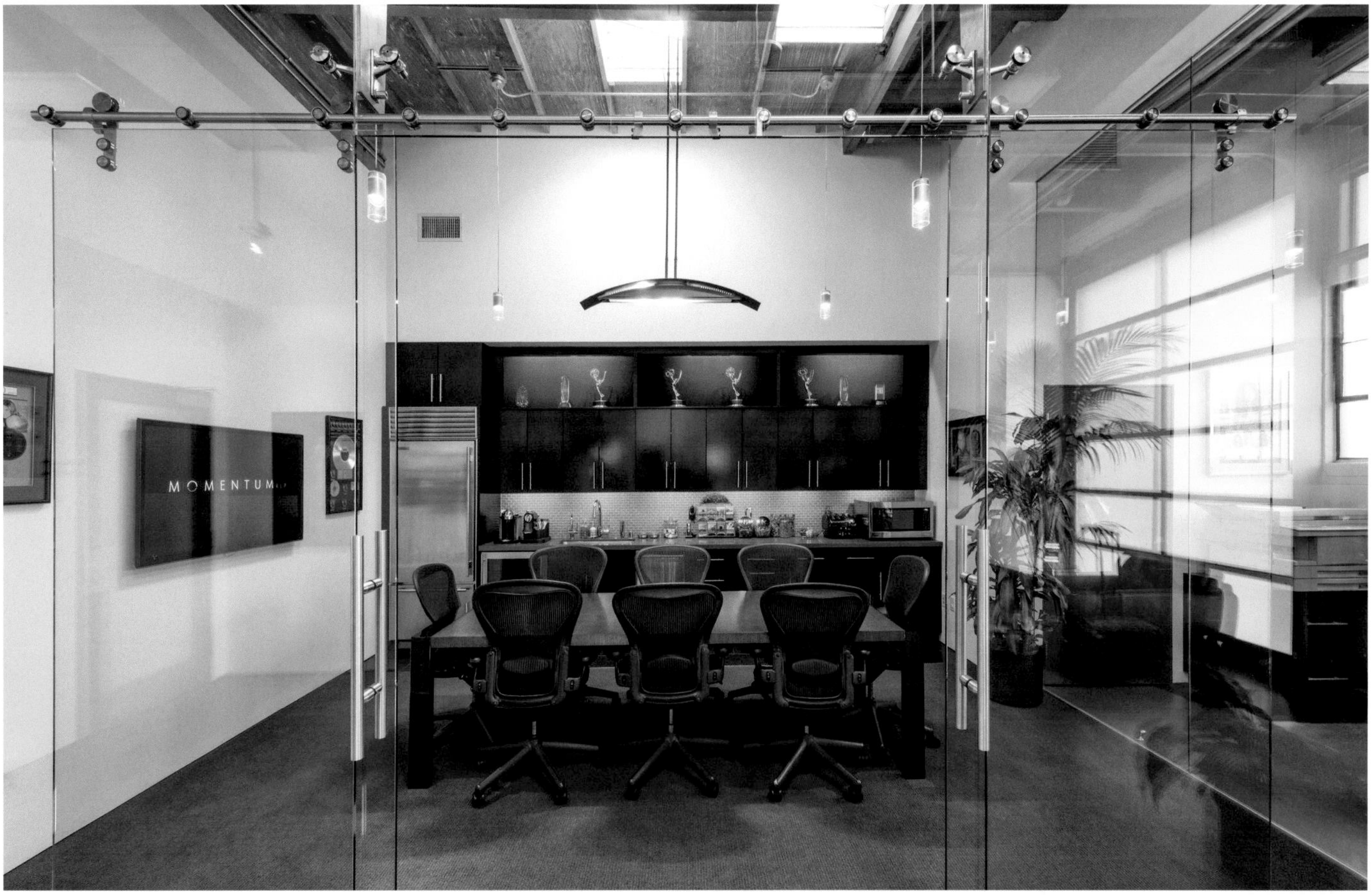
MOMENTUM

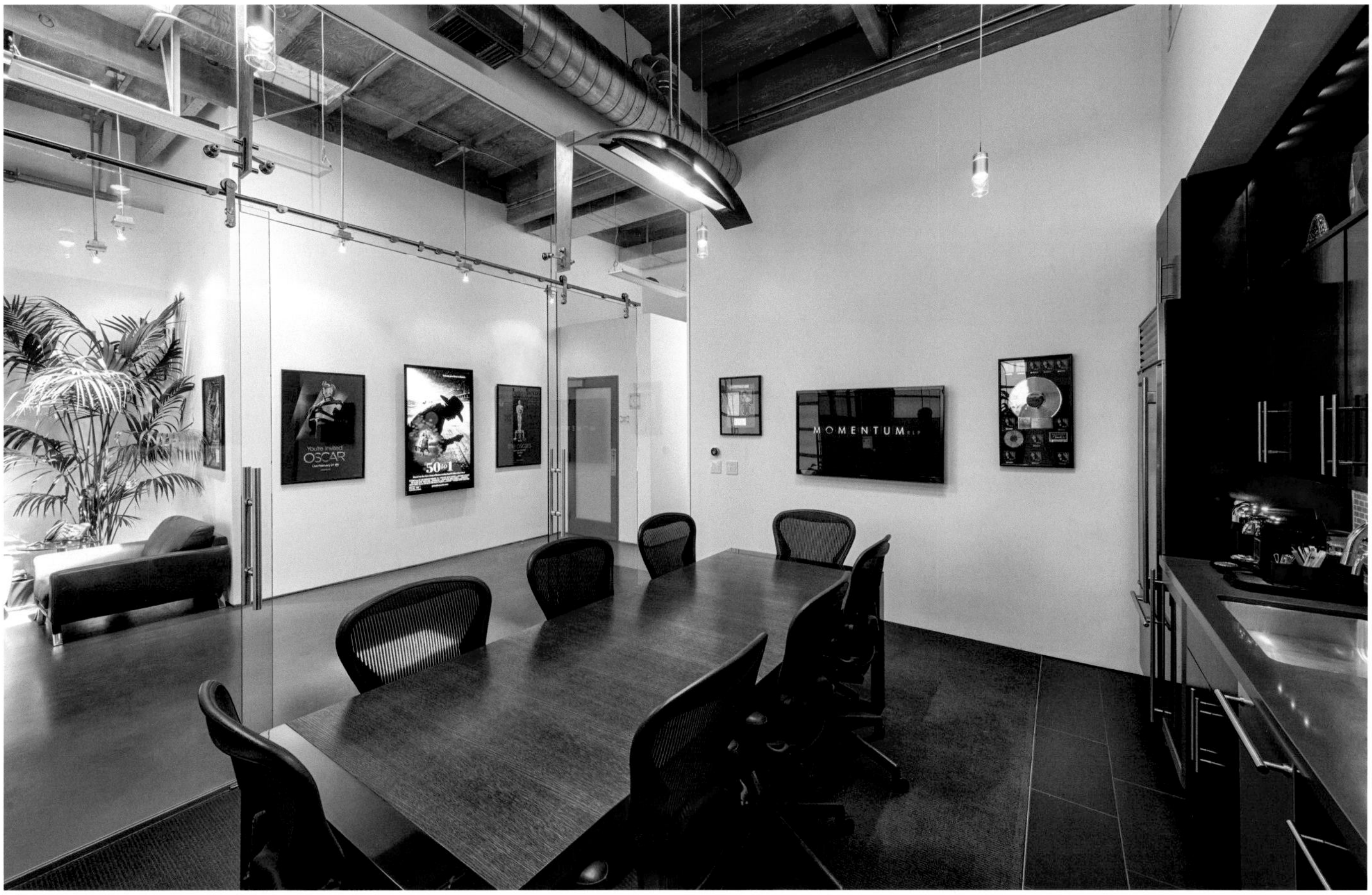
OSCAR
MOMENTUM

Momentum Hatteras

JNH Studios
Santa Monica, California

In 1997 studio bau:ton designed a 4,500 square foot recording studio for an acclaimed film composer in Santa Monica. Before it became a music composition and production facility, the building had already been converted from light-industrial use to a creative office space. The enclosed parking lot offered a rare opportunity for growth in this densely built-up area.

Over the past 20 years, several interior additions have further enhanced the scope and functionality of the facility. In 2005 a new composing suite was constructed in the rear of the building, some of the common areas received a facelift, and a basement was converted into a climate-controlled wine cellar.

Four years later, to keep up with technological advances, the main composing and mix room was remodeled. While the original had the feel of an audio mix room, the remodel focused on opening up the space and accommodating a large video display on the front wall. Removing a large equipment rack wall and reconfiguring the bass trapping in the rear yielded a comfortable seating area on a riser behind the composer's desk. The sloping wood ceiling was removed and replaced with level fabric surface. A cherry wood floor and wall paneling tie the room in to the aesthetic of the recently completed Studio B and warm-gray fabric panels complete the scheme. Custom acoustic diffusors that were used in the original scheme were either left in place or re-used in a modified layout. The main lounge areas were also updated and a large client area with bar and kitchen, connected to the outside with a glass rollup door, was added in the back of the building.

Ongoing explorations over the following years have included the potential addition of a second story, covered parking facilities and the redesign of the exterior Facade to a more contemporary and energy-efficient system. The latter is in progress now, along with a seismic upgrade of the roof structure.

SITE AND FLOOR PLAN

1 Studio
2 Overdub Booth
3 Sound Lock
4 Office
5 Kitchenette
6 Lounge
7 Gym
8 Restroom
9 Storage
10 Machine Room
11 Closet
12 Parking

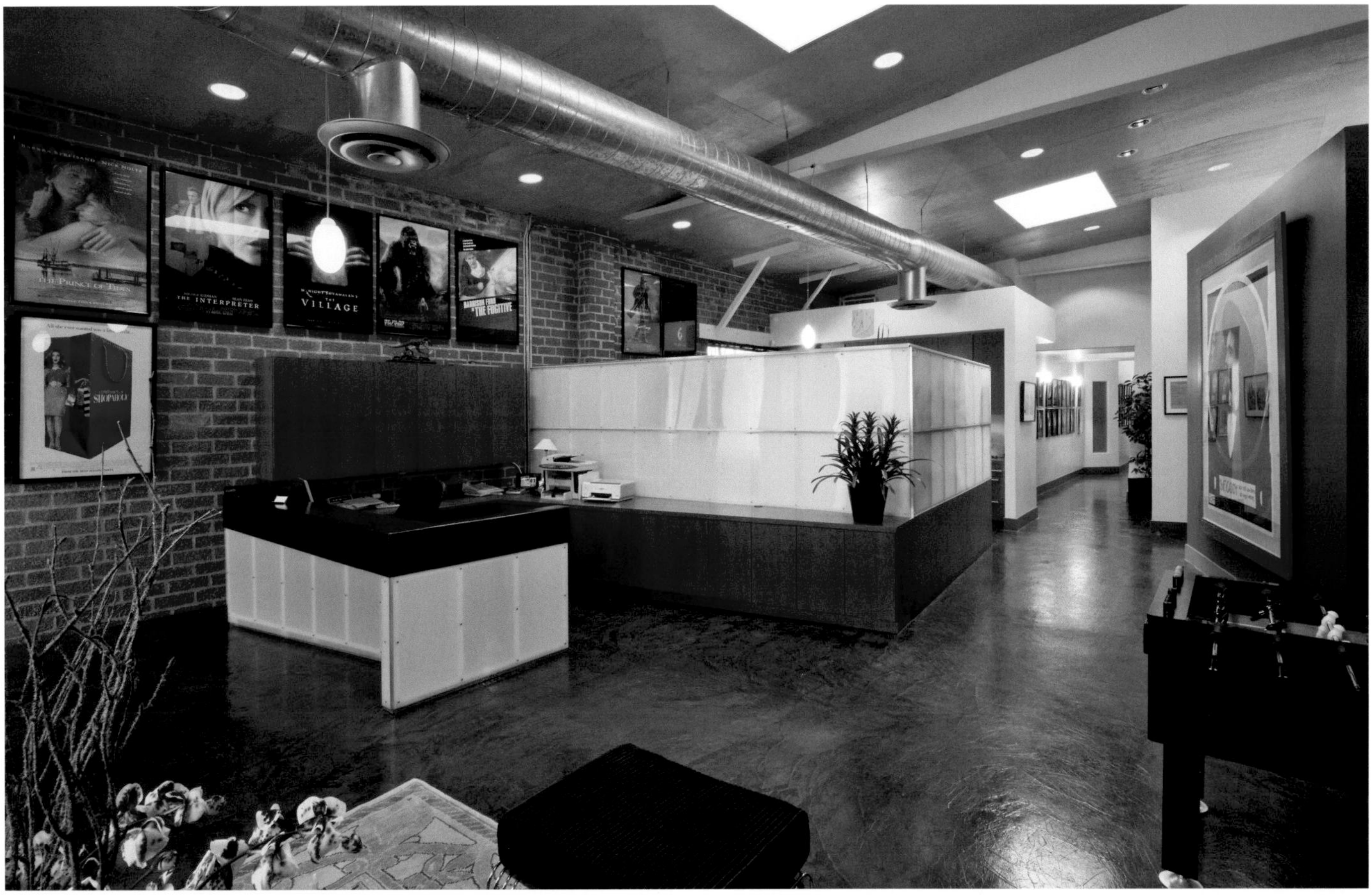

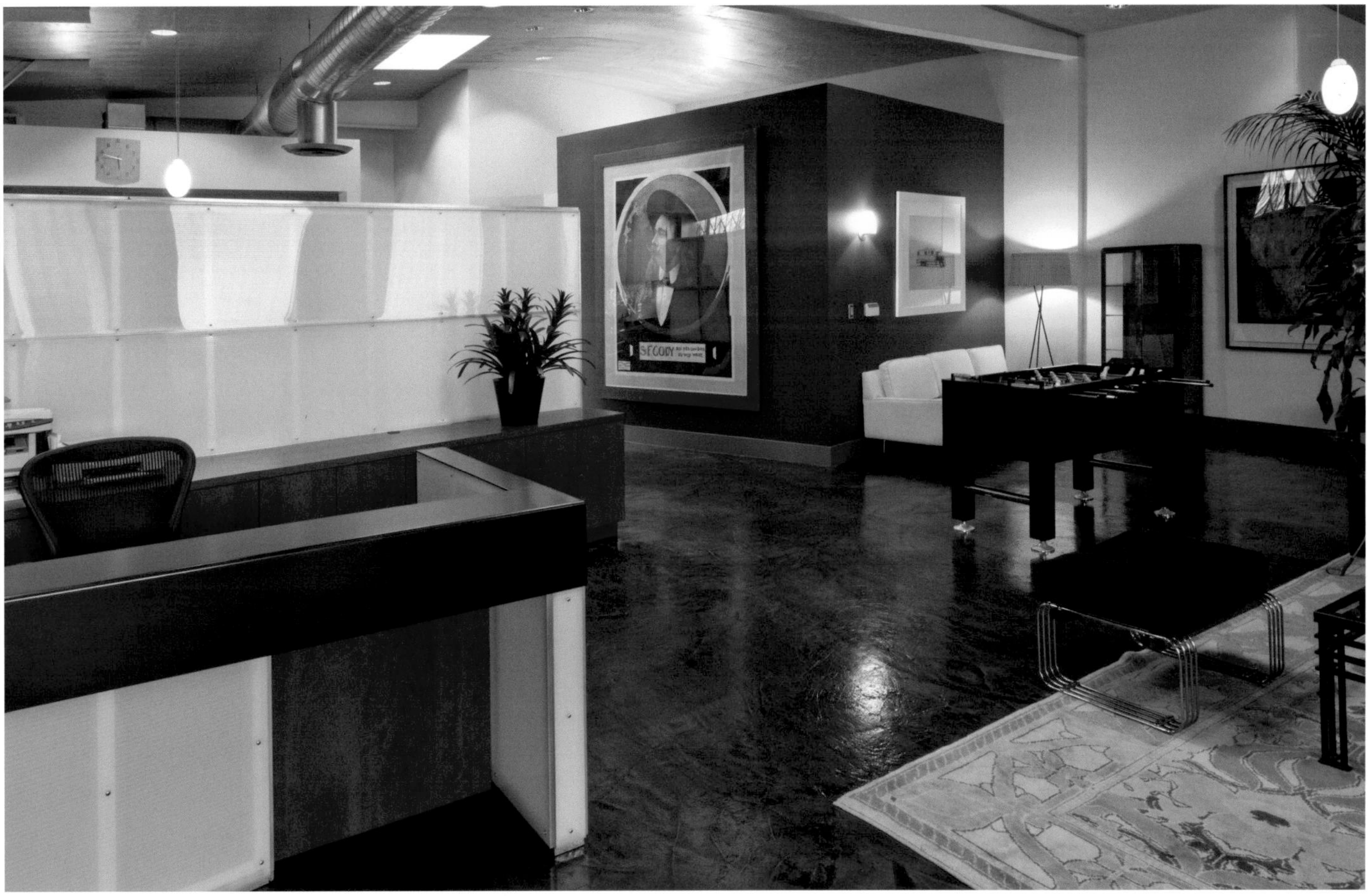

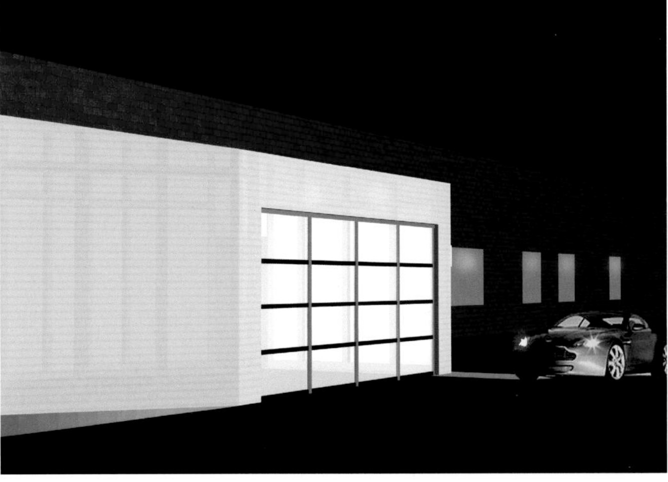

Garage Concept

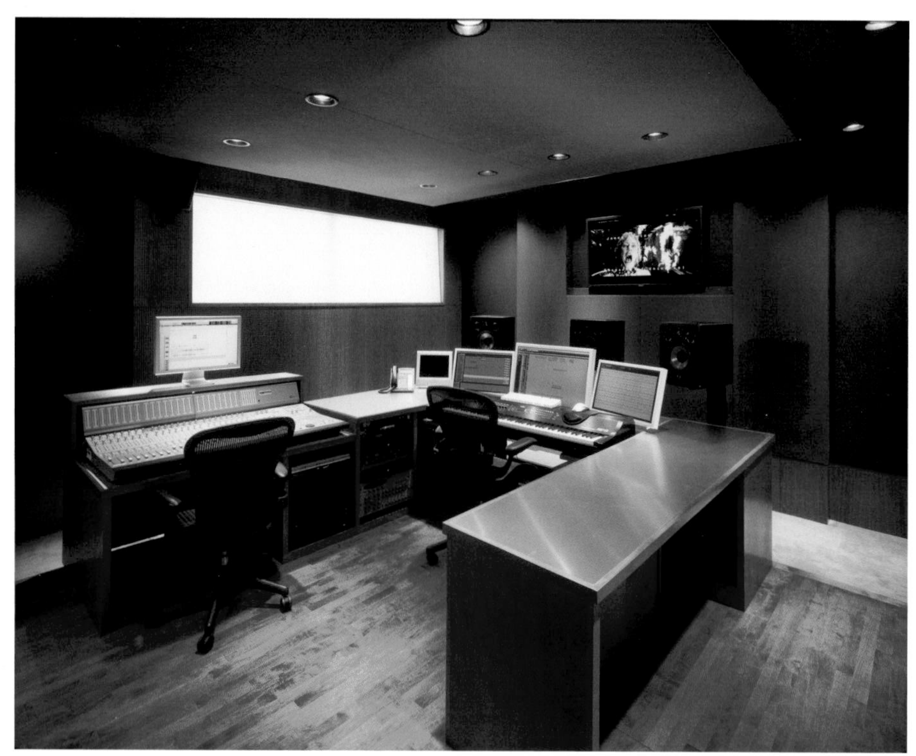

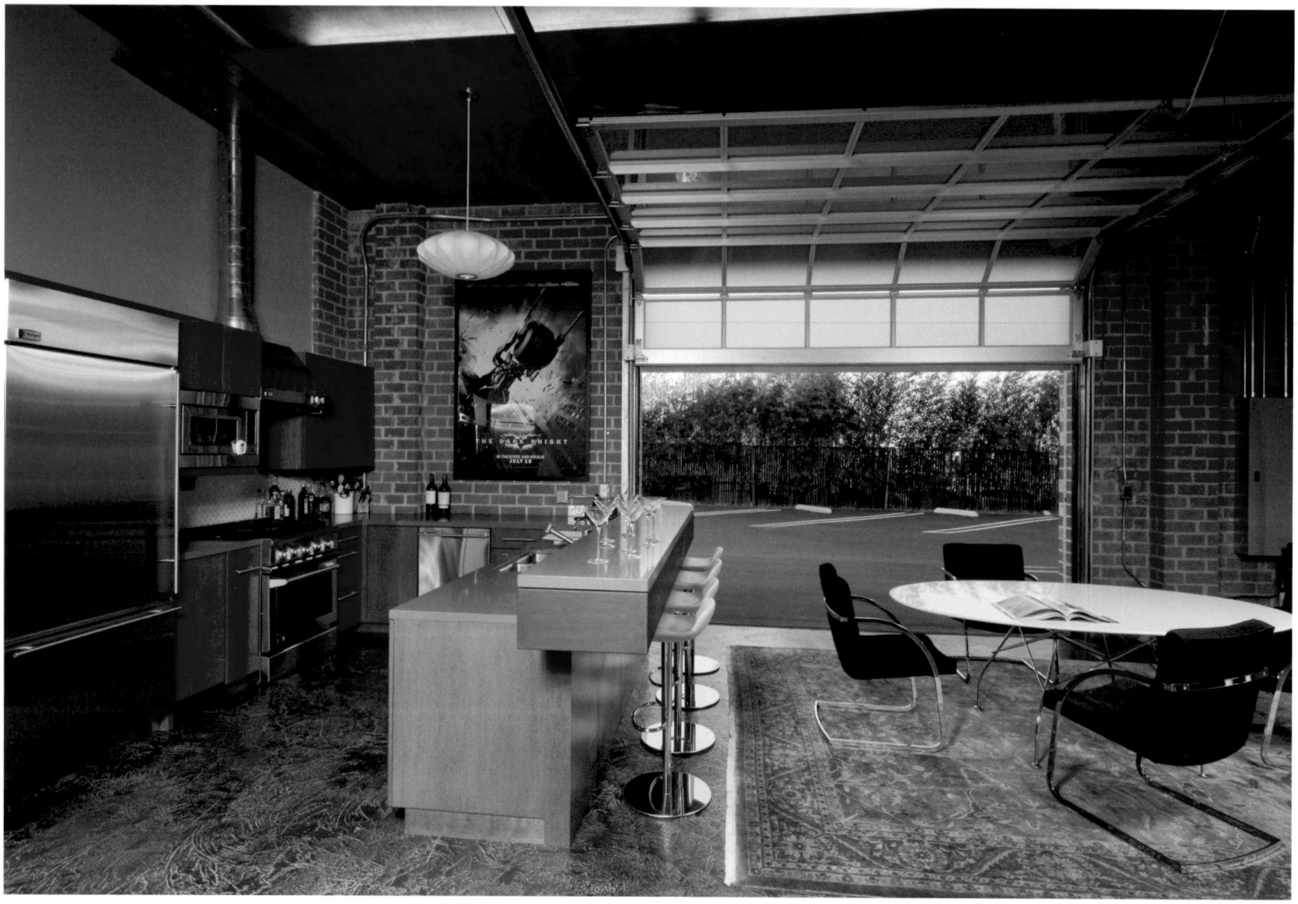
THE DARK KNIGHT
IN THEATERS AND IMAX
JULY 18

Q
QUESTED
VS2108

3 Capture

Fox Newman Scoring Stage, 2008

Atlantis, 2002

Montana Film, 2011

Boom Boom Room, 2004

Record Plant 1993

X-Art 1993

Sony Music, Tokyo 2001

Conversation
Bruce Botnick with David Goggin

DG You became famous as the recording engineer for The Doors. The story goes that the album *L.A. Woman* was recorded in a rehearsal space rather than in a traditional studio. Why did you record in a space without the acoustic treatment found in a recording studio?

BB When their producer Paul Rothchild decided that he couldn't bring anything more to their career and it was time for him to move on, they said, "What are we going to do?" And I said, "Well, where do you feel the most comfortable?" And they said, "In our rehearsal space." I said, "Great. I'll bring some remote gear in and we'll record there," and that was how it happened, and it actually worked out quite well. Their rehearsal room was jammed full of keyboards and Roby had a couple of amps, with Elvis's bass player Jerry Sheff and on rhythm guitar Marc Benno. Jim was standing in the bathroom, which was part of the room but had no door, so he'd stand there because that was the only place he could stand with a hand mic. We recorded the album all live, basically. We were lucky in the case of this album that they had been working in that space for years, so they knew it well. When they made a sound, I was able to capture that because my work is to capture what the musician does.

DG What is distinctive about your present private studio?

BB It's just the naturalness of it. I don't know technically what the decay times are and the resonance or anything like that. All I know is that it feels very comfortable, and when I have clients, or musicians, especially, they want to be in the room, and that's really something. I've been in a lot of control rooms and a lot of studios where that is not the case, where you walk in and the rooms are so trapped you feel like everything's being sucked out of your ears. This room breathes.

DG Visually, too, it's attractive, interesting. How important in your work is a place that's visually conducive to creativity?

BB I really love Peter's gift for making spaces that look and sound good as well. Not like the old days with lots of rock walls in the control room for diffusion and lots of absorption. I love the cleanliness of the design. To me, it's like being in a Bauhaus building that has that feeling of clarity. That's how I feel in the space; it doesn't intrude on me. Acoustically and visually, it's restful.

DG Most of your work these days is associated with visuals, movies and such. You have a big screen for your projects. Have the recordings that come to you been recorded with orchestras elsewhere?

BB I've recorded a fair amount of them, and then I either mix them on the scoring stage or mix them here in my studio synchronized to picture, with sixty or seventy tracks' worth of information and full surround.

DG You've worked with many composers, most notably, Jerry Goldsmith. How was that experience – the pressure and the creativity in those big rooms with those big orchestras, working with a top composer/conductor?

BB Recording orchestral scores for a movie is like when I started out. We only had three tracks available, so you had to get your balance and mix live. Moving into movies was right up my alley. I love recording large

110-piece orchestras with 20 or 30 tracks of electronics, and getting a live mix to print. The red light goes on, and you perform along with the orchestra.

DG What is your opinion about the way many recordings are done now? For an album project, in many cases, the artists never see each other. They do their track in one studio; they send it to another guy. It's very different than capturing this massive live sound at once with a group of human beings.

BB They are missing out! It's like when you go to a movie theater. You're with a theater full of people, and they're emotionally reacting to what's up on the screen, and you feel that energy. When you're in the studio, you've got the band and the singer, and the engineer and arranger in the control room, and they're all working together. They're all experiencing that performance as a whole. To not have that seems sad.

DG Do you think that the sound of digital is finally as good or equivalent to analog?

BB At very high resolutions, I think it's close. We're still not there, but it's close.

DG You're also a photographer, and you've lived through the transition from traditional film processing to digital. The equivalent is happening in your audio world. Some people are still going back to film, though. What's going on?

BB It's a desire, especially for people that have recorded on analog tape. A lot of them have been there before, and they like what it does.

DG You've also been involved with Neil Young on a consumer plan for lossless high-resolution digital music. Meanwhile, most people are still listening to MP3s on smartphones.

BB Neil has always wanted to present his and other artists' music in studio quality so that what we hear in the studio you can hear in your home. He conceived of Pono, and developed a high resolution player that fit in your hand, and it worked and sounded really great. Unfortunately, the company didn't survive the vicissitudes of time, but it was a great effort to try and bring high-resolution to the listeners. Today Neil is taking it a little further on his website. He's streaming all his music and Crosby, Stills, Nash & Young, Buffalo Springfield

Bruce Botnick with Mr. Bonzai

UnitEye studio in Ojai

and Crazy Horse, and any other act that he was involved with, without any data compression and full high resolution up to 192k/24 bit. And when people hear and feel the music as it was intended, they understand it.

When I was teaching at USC, we'd always have a live band come in, either a jazz band or classical, from the Thornton School of Music. We'd set up a studio, and I would get the initial balance and make sure it was right. Then the students could sit down and have their ten minutes at the console to either move the faders around or just sit there and listen.

One kid sat down, and he didn't touch anything. He just listened. And when he was done, he started to get up but collapsed, and I grabbed him, and sat him down. I said, "Are you okay?" He said, "I've never heard sound that clear before." It's an MP3 generation, and it's a matter of education.

DG You've worked with Peter previously on a Neutra house that you lived in, which must be a very specialized type of work in keeping true to the original architecture.

BB When we were restoring and remodeling our Neutra home, we talked extensively with Peter about restoring and updating and expanding the original design and remaining true to the intent. It's not just what it looks like, but also it's how it's executed, and how it goes together. It's the things you don't see in the design that are the most important part, sort of like the music that we make. It's the visualization of the architectural design and the visualization of sound in music; they go hand in hand.

A lot of the time, when I'm recording, I'm not looking at the meters; I'm not looking at the orchestras; I'm not looking at the picture on the screen. I'm listening. Many kids today, they look at the computer screen and make changes by what they're looking at,; they aren't listening. I said, "Turn that off. Use your ears, please. Listen."

DG This room is purposely isolated from the real world.

BB Yes, this room is a room within a larger room. The studio floor that we're sitting on is on a separated pad. It's floating. The walls are here, but this room does not touch that side over there, to avoid transmission of sounds. I have a neighbor next door, and I could have my 21-inch subwoofer pounding massive explosions of bass, but they never even know I'm here. To keep the room isolated and have it sound good is masterful black magic.

A home tells you how you can live in it, and I would say that, even in the studio, it's true. I spend more time in the studio than I do at home, so it's home. But having lived in an architectural home, and now having moved away from it, we have a better understanding of it. Richard Neutra used to go to a site, and he would spend days there watching the light, how it'd fall, and where the view changes, and what would happen, and the traffic, and then he would site the house, accordingly.

Our home was designed in 1947, and the restoration that we undertook was a different take on things. It's like what I'm doing here today on this Doors *Soft Parade* album and mixing new stuff that people haven't heard before. I can't go back to 1969 in my head. I can't do it. This is 2019, and so I approach things a lot differently, and I figure that's valid.

Architecturally and emotionally, bringing modernism into your life is good; because of the amount of clarity it gives you in your life.

DG You've got to have an environment that feels comfortable, but effective for the music that you are making. Could you conclude with some thoughts about the results of your relationship with Peter?

BB We had a mid-century architectural home, and it not only tells you how you can live in it, it tells you what you can do with it. You want to keep the aesthetic, and not change it so much that it's no longer the original concept of the original architect. It's all about communication and understanding, and listening more than anything else, listening to one another and communicating and being clear about the goal. The house was telling us what we could and couldn't do, and Peter totally got it.

DG You have a skylight here in your recording studio.

BB This is one of the things that we talked about. I've spent so many years in a cave, in a control room, with no sense of day or night. We couldn't have windows here, but I could have a skylight. I wanted some natural light to make me feel better about being here, because there's something about natural light that cheers you up. And as evening falls, it gets darker, and now that I'm older, I don't really like working at night. So it gets dark, and it's time to go home.

Bruce Botnick is an audio engineer and producer and the previous owner, with his wife Marie, of the Pacific Palisades Neutra residence and the current owner of his UnitEye studio in Ojai.

Windmark

Santa Monica, California

When the current owner bought the building that was to house this new studio suite, it already contained an operational recording facility. A respected multi-instrumentalist musician, songwriter, producer, and former Virginia Beach studio owner, he was planning to build a studio for his own projects and let his grown children run the overall facility as a commercial studio for hire.

The existing studios in the building had been placed on the upper floor of the steel-framed building, not on the relatively solid ground floor, on a concrete slab over the parking garage. The steel's acoustically conductive properties enabled the sound vibrations from the studios to easily travel within the building's structure. The older studios had been designed and built with marginal knowledge of acoustics. With no comprehensive soundproofing concept, there were a number of severe sound leaks between the two floors and the studios themselves. As a result, the playback of hip hop and rock music with loud bass frequencies, a main objective of the new ownership's studio clientele, was impossible. Leaking sound rattled equipment, ceilings, and walls on the floor below. In addition to the preexisting soundproofing issues, space constraints in the floor plan, as well as low ceilings with minimal space for ducting, compounded the acoustic isolation concerns.

During the first phase of the new project, an additional recording booth was added to one of the existing second floor studio suites. Taking advantage of the natural light, the booth features a large frosted window and customized suspended wood diffuser panels on the ceiling.

The challenging site and the owner's passion for rare vintage equipment and the analog recording process, with its unmistakable sound, were all instrumental in guiding the design of the new studio on the floor below. Inspired by iconic rock 'n roll studios from the 60s and 70s in both the aesthetics of the spaces and the equipment it houses, the design was re-interpreted to satisfy contemporary technical needs and aesthetics.

Since it was not feasible to improve the soundproofing of the existing rooms, the new construction had to compensate for the lack of isolation. The need to rigorously soundproof the added studio from the existing facility required an elaborate air conditioning ducting system, which then informed the layout and the shapes of the ceiling soffits. Turning a potentially serious problem into an asset, the ducting runs were fine-tuned and the ceiling layout closely tailored to the required duct volumes. The spatial modulations required by the room acoustics and the mechanical system were balanced to accommodate both.

The walnut, bamboo, and fabric finishes are complemented by an array of color-changing LED light fixtures. A main feature of the design, the lights permit the creation of a finely customized visual atmosphere and allow users to control the mood in each of the different spaces. A subdued natural color scheme serves as the backdrop for an immersive and customizable vibe, aiding the creative process of making different kinds of music.

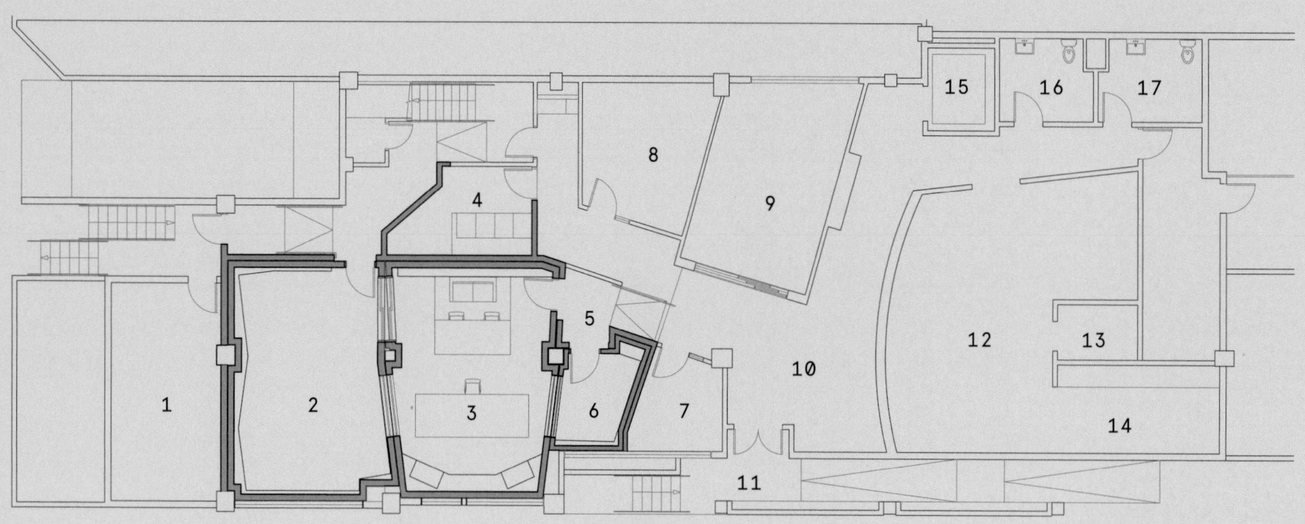

GROUND FLOOR PLAN

1	Terrace	10	Reception
2	Tracking Room	11	Entry
3	Control Room	12	Lounge
4	CMR	13	Storage
5	Vestibule	14	Kitchen
6	Booth	15	Elevator
7	Office	16	Men's Restroom
8	Producer	17	Women's Restroom
9	Conference	18	Trash

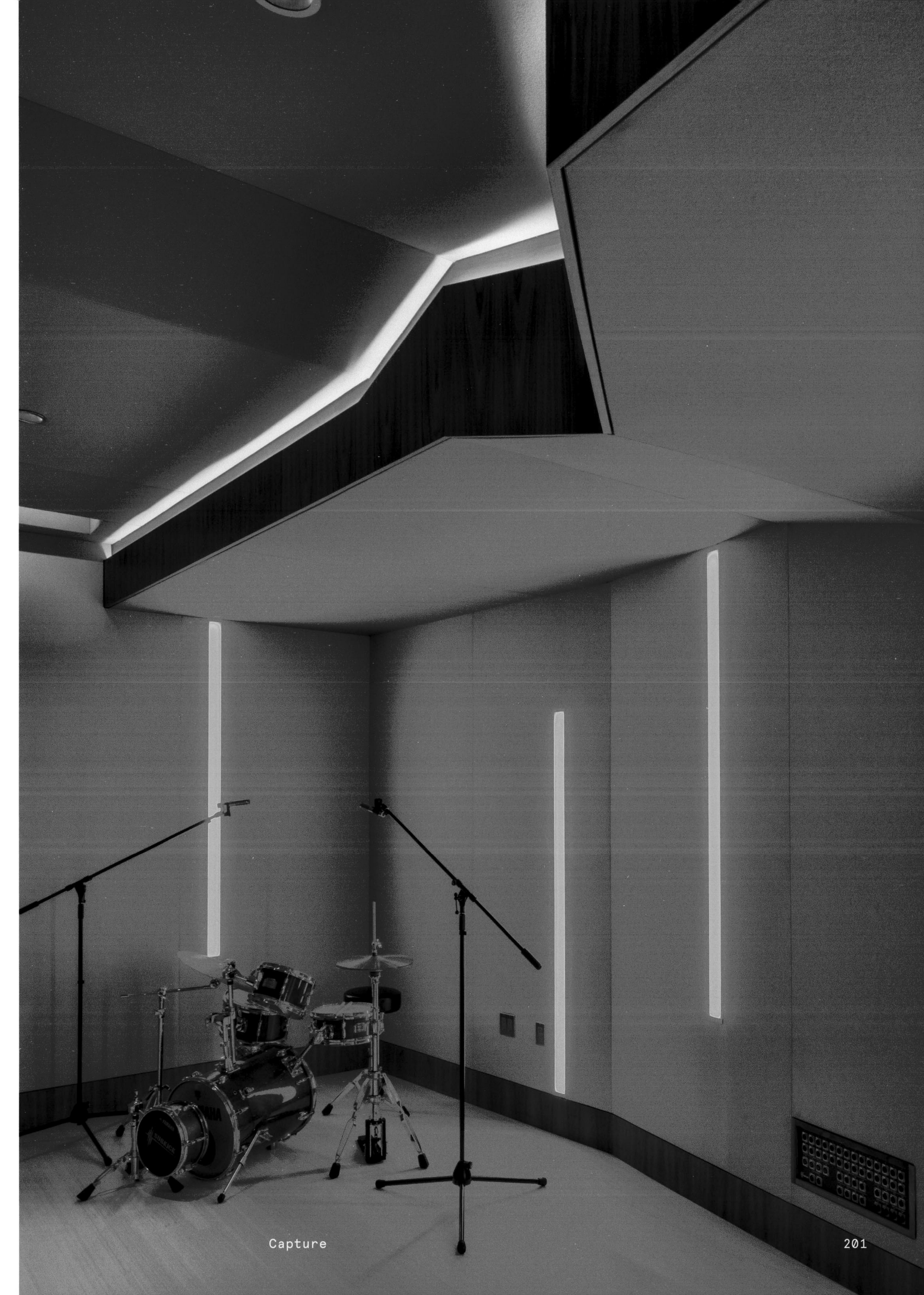

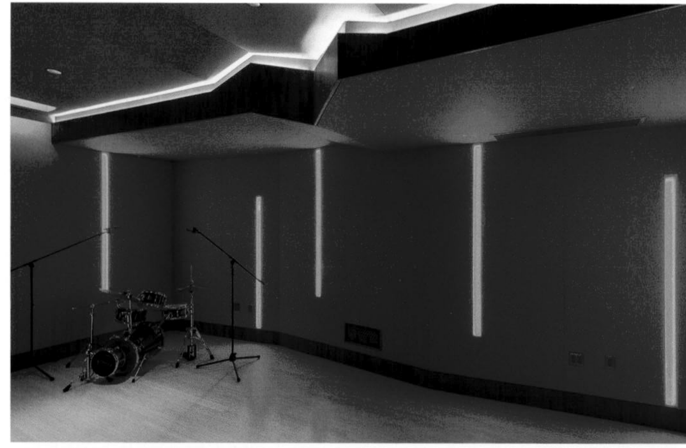

Second floor recording booth

DreamWorks
Glendale, California

DreamWorks Animation SKG had occupied a lush, Tuscan-inspired campus in Glendale for over a decade when it decided in 2010 to add an in-house recording studio and movie premix stage on its premises. Besides the flagship voice recording studio and the fully equipped mix stage, the new facility also contains sound edit rooms, as well as green room and videoconferencing facilities.

Incorporating the studios on its campus has resulted in significant timesavings, has cut back on executive and talent travel across town, and has enhanced the overall production workflow for the prolific animation studio.

The facility's location in the basement of a recently added office building expansion posed spatial challenges that were solved with a complex three-dimensional puzzle of single- and double-height spaces. The close proximity of acoustically sensitive rooms, both in plan and vertically in section, required a carefully developed space planning concept and extensive soundproofing measures. The project was initially started as part of the office addition, but then put on hold for over a year. When it resumed, the plan had to be reconfigured to satisfy new requirements and emerged quite different from the original scheme.

Voice recordings for animated feature films are typically done early in the filmmaking process, with actors working with preliminary visuals. This allows the voice talent to be filmed and the animation itself to be tailored to their acting during their vocal performances. Consequently, not only the sonic environment, but also the video capabilities of the space are important. Permanently installed and discretely disguised video cameras and adjustable lighting are positioned to capture every aspect and each mannerism of the actors voicing the animated characters.

The eighteen-foot-tall main recording room features suspended ceiling clouds that serve as acoustical components. They also conceal air ducts and lighting and add a strong visual element. The room is equipped with film projection ports from the large server room on the upper floor. Film projections are used for added automated dialogue replacement (ADR) functions.

The adjacent control room is connected to the recording space with a large window and direct access through a dedicated sound lock. Besides the generous seating and technical installations, a producer's booth in the back provides privacy and quiet during sessions.

The mix stage across the hall is used for preliminary sound mixes but is capable of producing entire film mixes if needed. Sound editing in the six adjacent edit rooms complements the stages, and a central machine room contains the technical infrastructure serving all of the new facility.

The studio's location in the basement and at the edge of the campus facilitates private access for celebrity clients and maintains secrecy during the many-years-long long effort of producing animated films.

BASEMENT FLOOR PLAN

1 Control Room
2 Voice Recording
3 Pre-Mixing
4 Pantry
5 Sound Lock
6 Storage
7 Sound Edit
8 Producer's Room
10 Pump Room
11 Hallway
12 Back-of-house-pantry
13 Equipment Room
14 VTC Room
15 Restroom

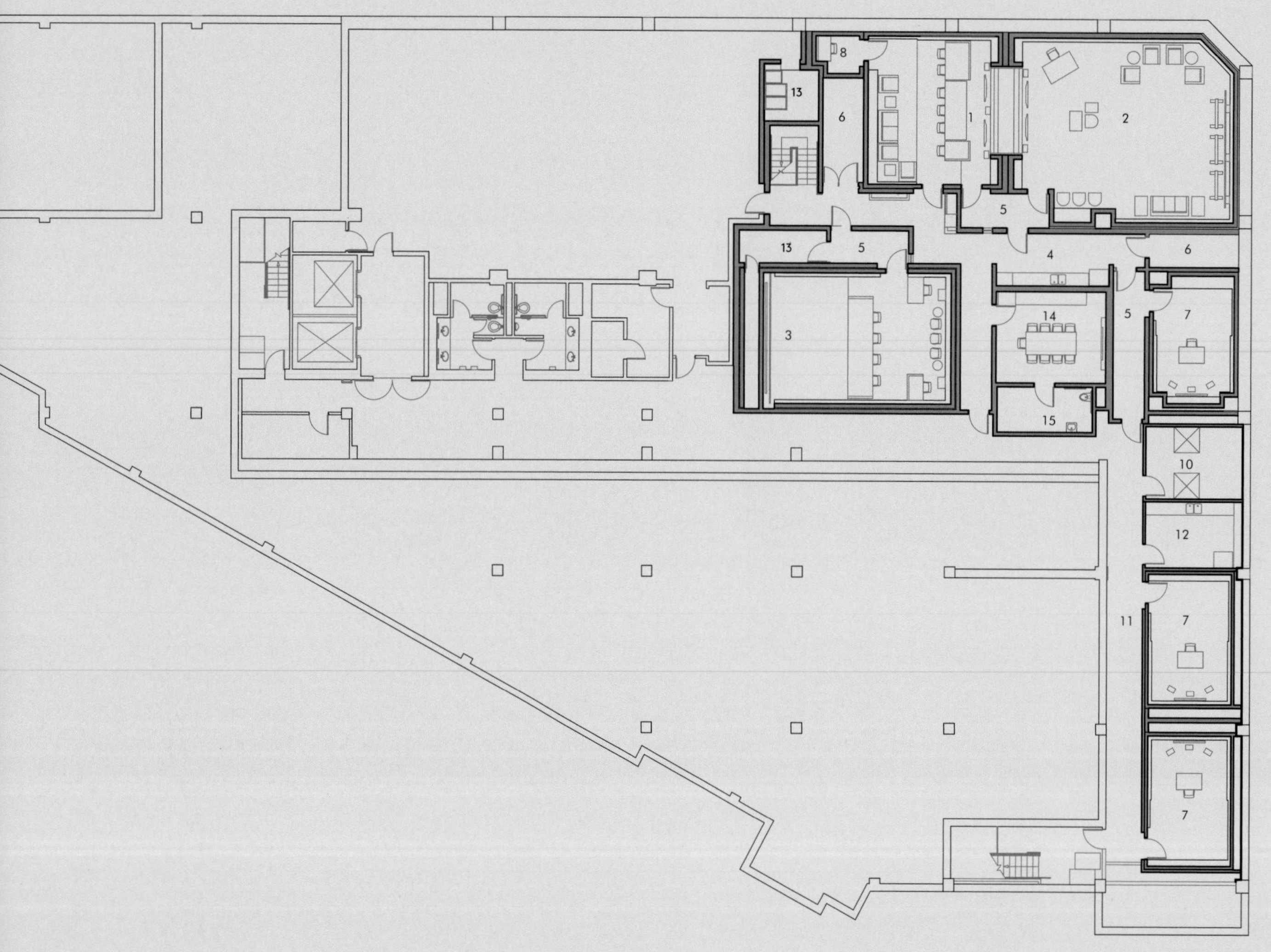

DREAMWORKS
DREAMWORKS

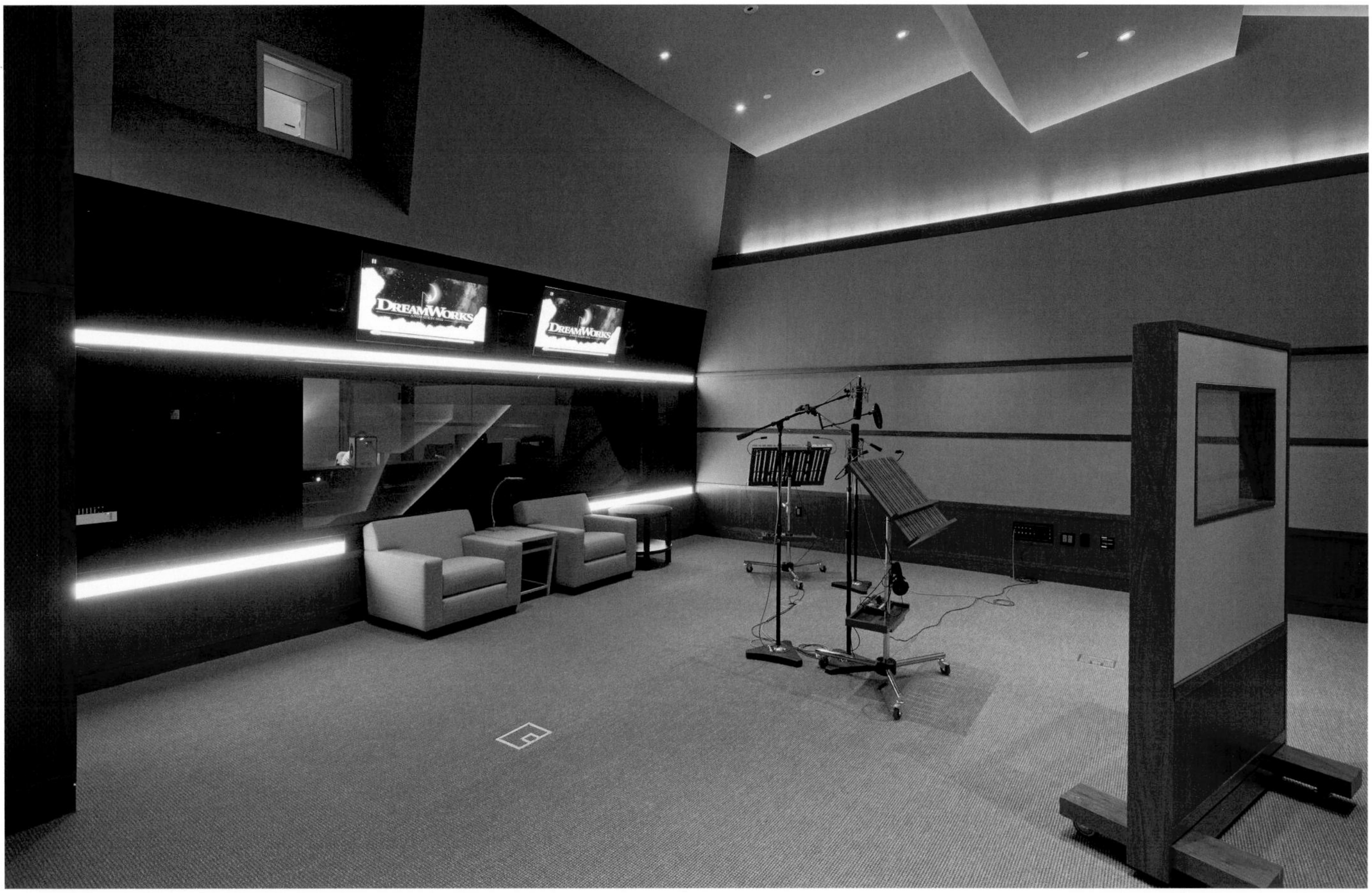
DREAMWORKS
DREAMWORKS

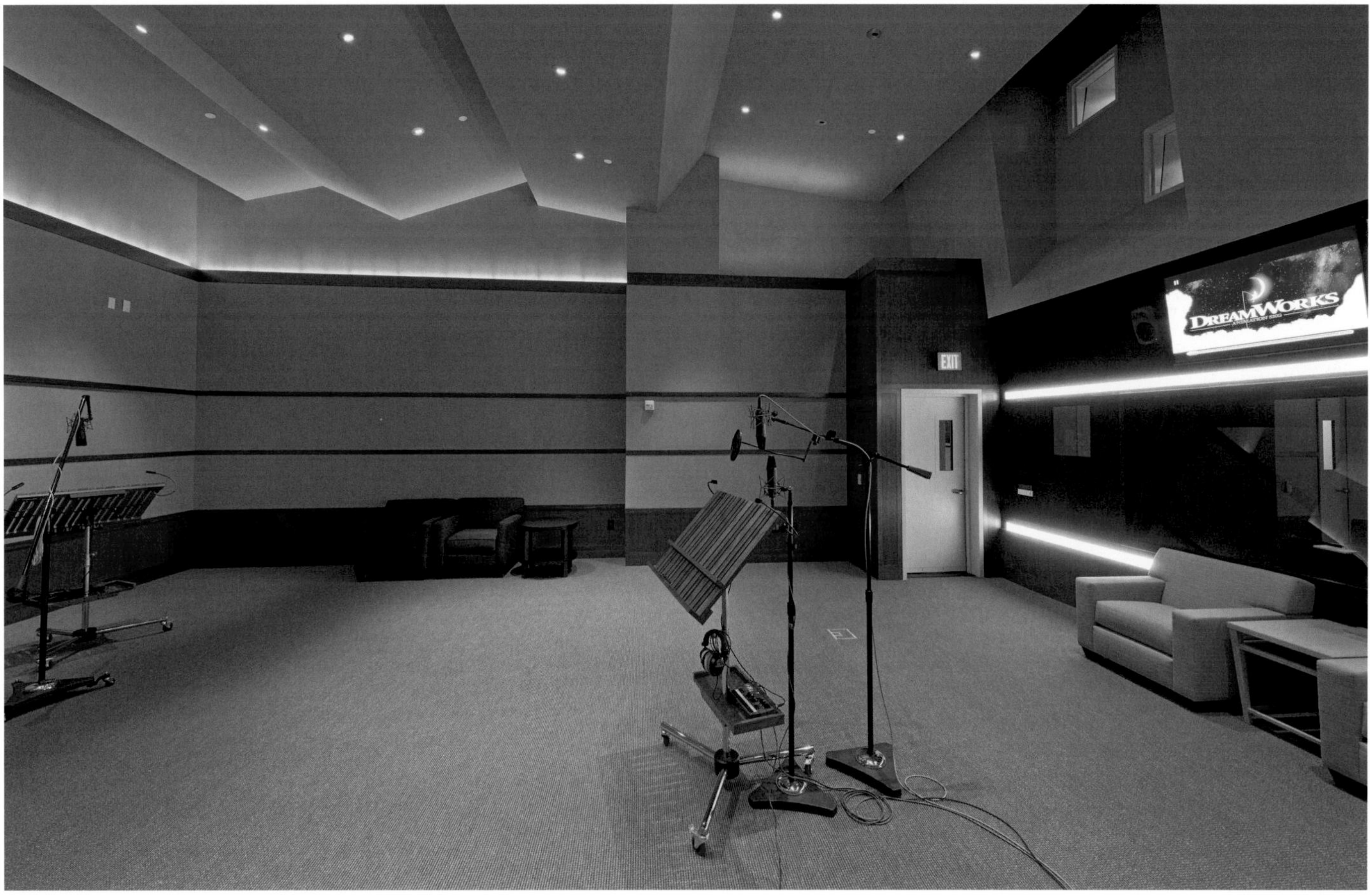
EXIT
DREAMWORKS

DREAMWORKS
DREAMWORKS

Mix Stage

Red Amp Audio
Richmond, Virginia

This multi-use media production facility is located in a commercial building along a main artery in downtown Richmond, the state capital of Virginia. The storefront building was originally built in 1938, and its front facade was listed as historically significant by the city. Over the years the building has housed an appliance showroom, a jewelry store, a disco, a record label, and most recently, a photography studio. An open double-height space in the center of the floor plan made it appealing as a location for a recording studio.

9WG Studios, named after its street address, includes Red Amp Audio, the recording studio component, as well as TV and postproduction features. The studio now features two audio recording suites, a tall tracking room with an isolation booth, two edit suites, and a green-screen cyclorama or cyc wall room. The owners wanted to create a place that would function as a haven for freelance graphic designers, mixers, editors, videographers, and photographers alike. This approach allows the studio to function as a full service facility or as a space for independent contractors.

To accommodate all these uses on a relatively low budget, a nontraditional approach was necessary. Although the project was put on hold for a year while funding applications for historical facade preservation were pending, that financial support ultimately didn't materialize. As a result, the project found itself both delayed and without the anticipated extra funds.

Accordingly, the existing spatial configuration had to be utilized without any major structural modifications to fit a puzzle of intricately connected spaces while providing the best possible sound isolation and acoustic environment.

With the use of local wood, cotton insulation, bamboo floors, and vibrant paint colors, the environmentally friendly construction resulted in spaces that were meant to feel warm yet provide a creative spark. Economical, off-the-shelf materials were carefully arranged for acoustic performance with less of the preciousness or technical wizardry often found in similar projects. The formal language of the simple palette is spatially and visually emphasized with a few subtle twists and angles that concurrently reinforce the acoustic concept of the spaces by providing diffusion, low frequency absorption, and aimed deflections. To complement the overall concept of the building and the production spaces, the Richmond firm of Glavé & Holmes designed the common areas in the building.

The owners, prominent artists and members of the thriving local music scene, have made sure the studio never sits idle, and live recordings are constantly booked. At the same time, the facility has become a regular stop on the monthly First Fridays Art Walk event, opening up to visitors of the Richmond Arts District.

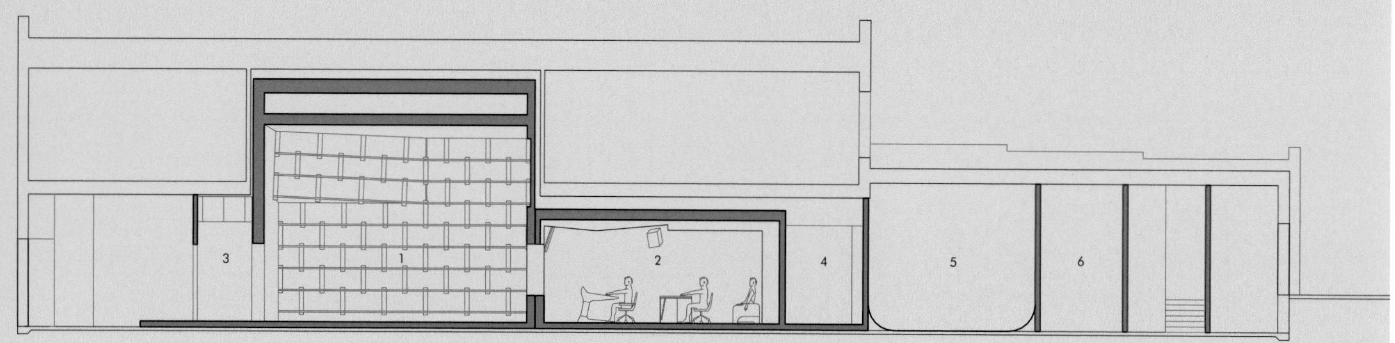

SECTION

1 Studio/Tracking Room
2 Mix Room A
3 Sound Lock
4 Central Machine Room
5 Video Stage
6 Kitchenette

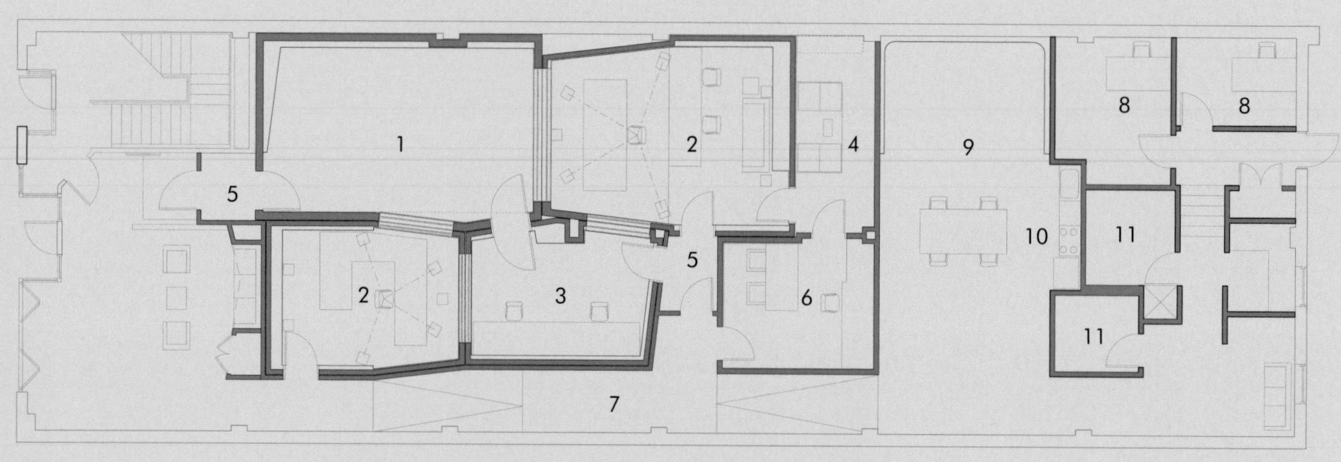

GROUND FLOOR PLAN

1 Studio/Tracking Room
2 Mix Room
3 Iso Room
4 Central Machine Room
5 Sound Lock
6 Editing Room
7 Hallway
8 Office
9 Video Stage
10 Kitchenette
11 Bathroom

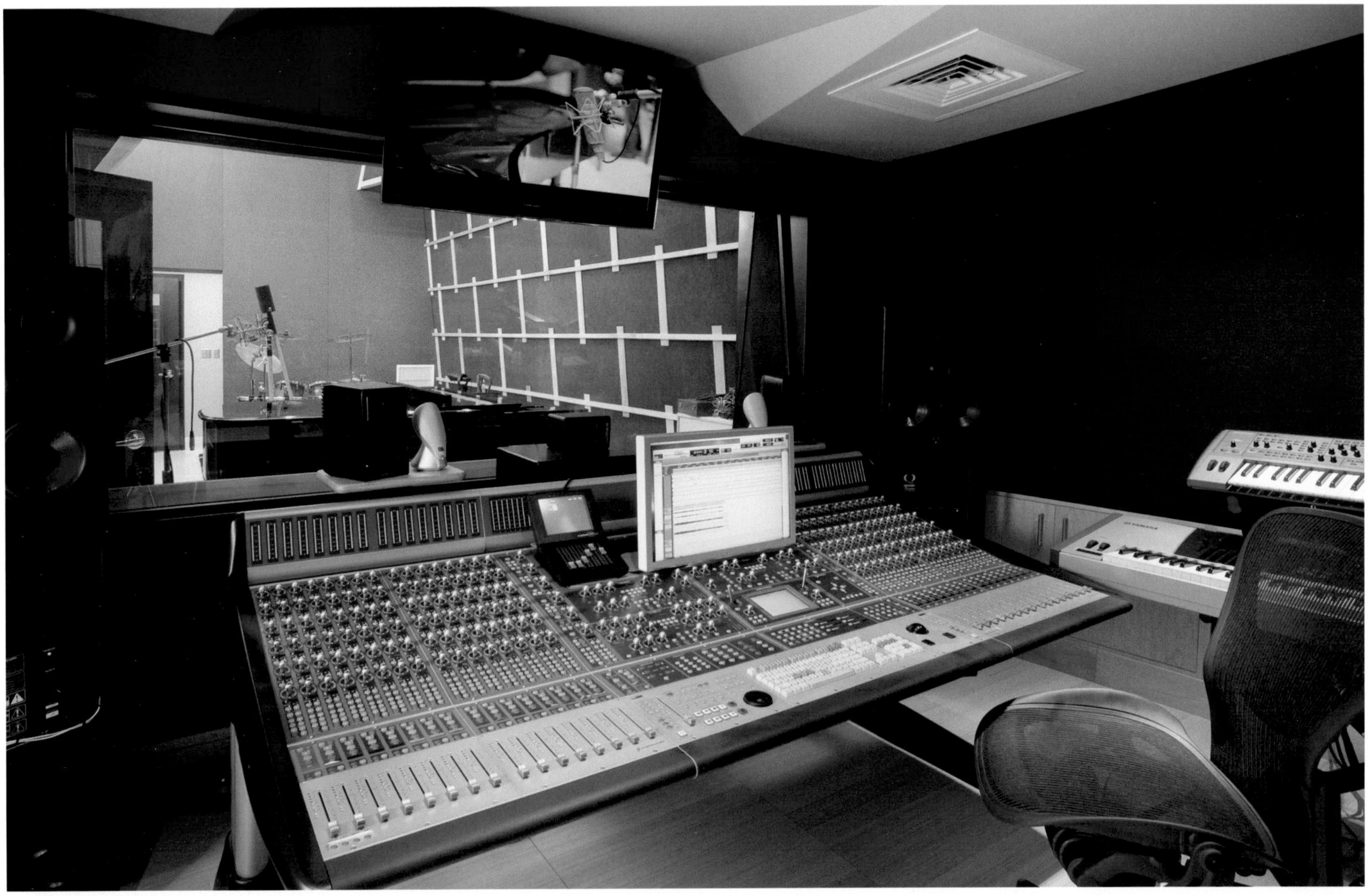

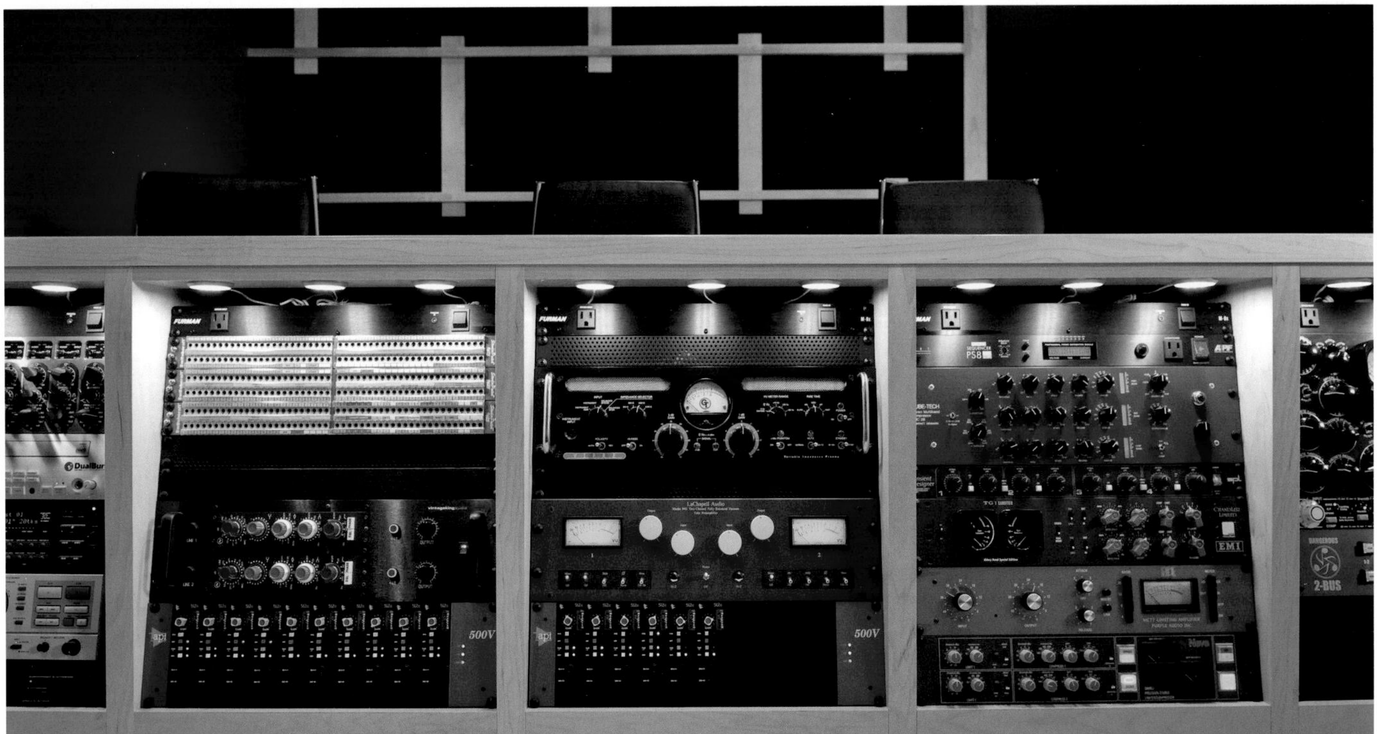
FURMAN
FURMAN
500V
500V
EMI
2-BUS

Gibraltar
YAMAHA

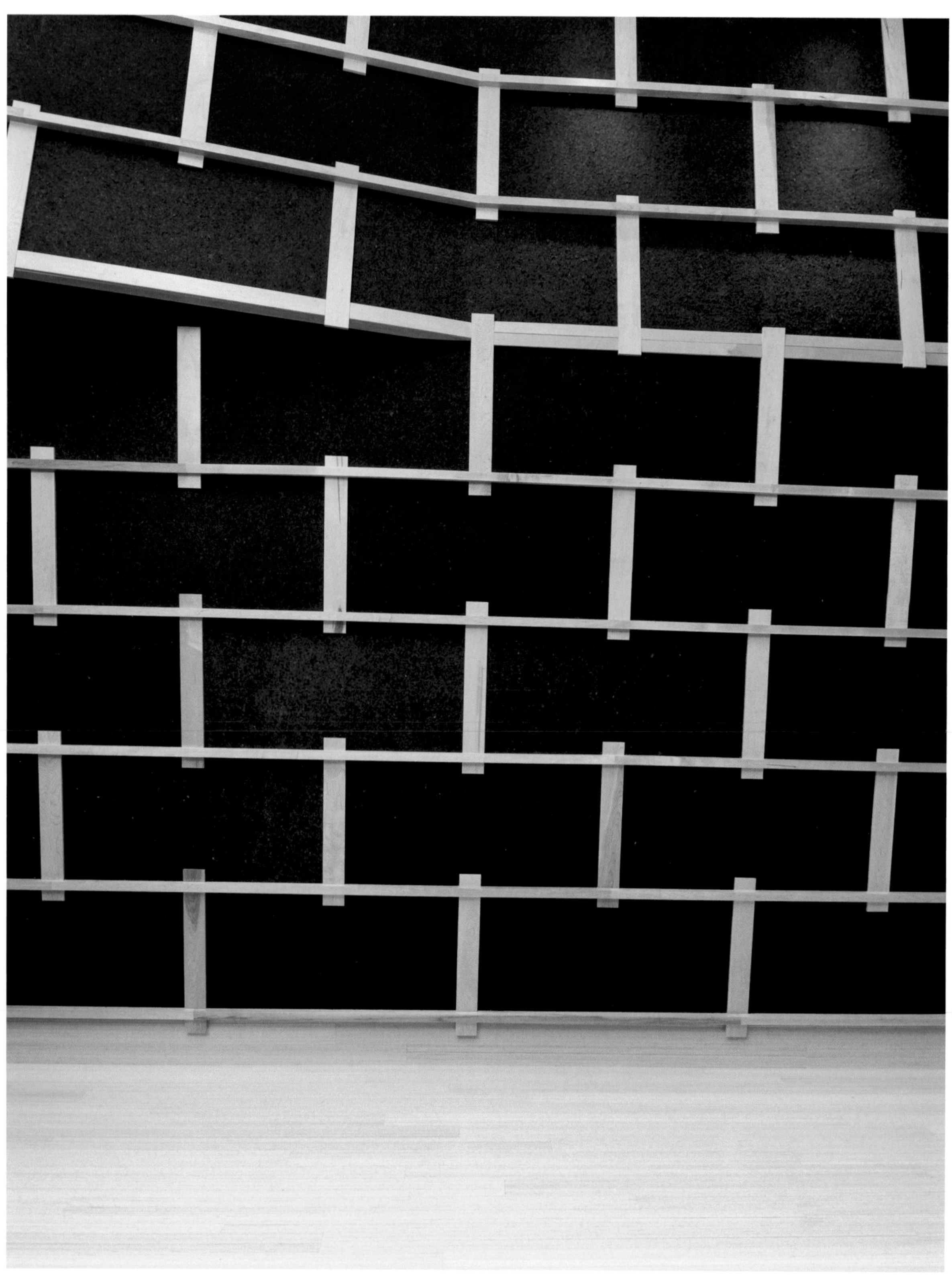

Cahuenga

Los Angeles, California

The owner, a drummer and music producer, had been using a small residence along the Melrose corridor in Los Angeles as a recording studio and production space for a few years. It was located in a commercial zone and being operated as a small commercial studio. The corner lot was to be developed for better use with a three-story commercial building, incorporating larger studios and production facilities. The goal was to replace the small and outdated spaces with a larger and better version and to add much needed amenities.

The required parking was placed on the ground floor, with two levels of studios, offices, and lounges floating over it. A large roof deck was to complement the lounge and office areas on the top level and offer views to the Hollywood Hills and the surrounding city.

The interior shapes of the studio walls are reflected on the exterior facade, a triangulated concrete plane that modulates the relatively large volume. A required fire exit was turned into a sculptural exterior element.

Due to the difficulties of finding a replacement studio during the lengthy construction period on the site of the current building, the project was eventually abandoned. Instead, an adjacent warehouse was purchased and converted to a studio facility, while the operations in the original house could continue. With the planned program for this project now in place next door, alternate development options are being considered.

SECOND FLOOR PLAN

1 Mix Room
2 Tracking Room
3 Iso Booth
4 Sound Lock
5 Lounge
6 Kitchen
7 Equipment Room
8 Restroom

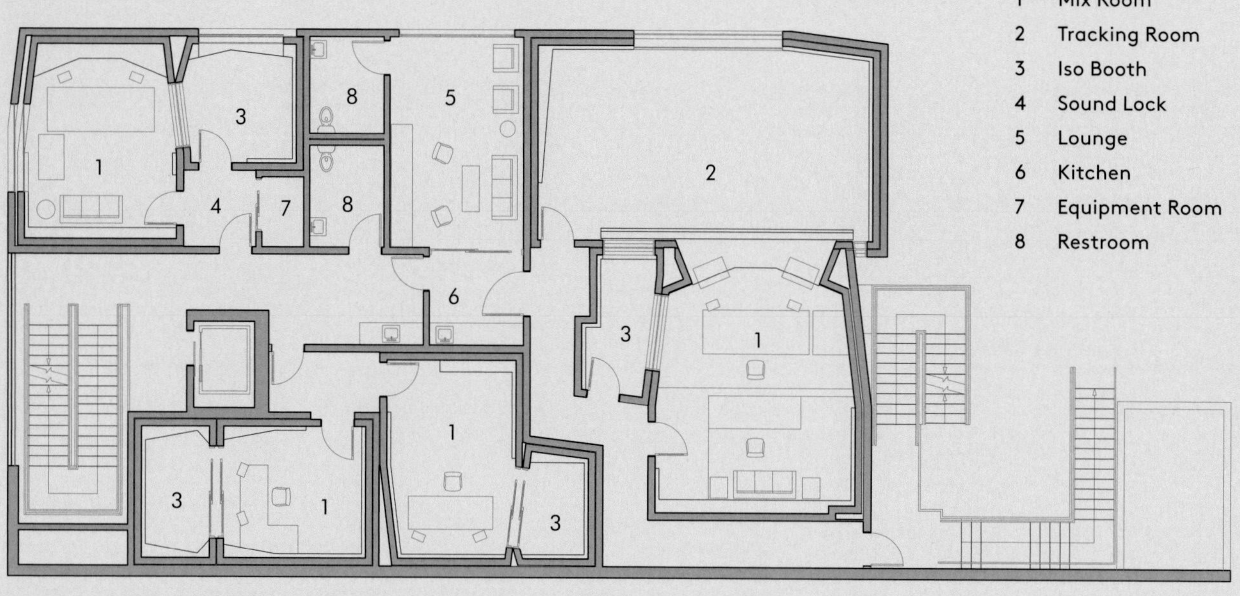

THIRD FLOOR PLAN

1 Office
2 Conference
3 Lounge
4 Deck
5 Storage
6 Mechanical Equipment
7 Restroom

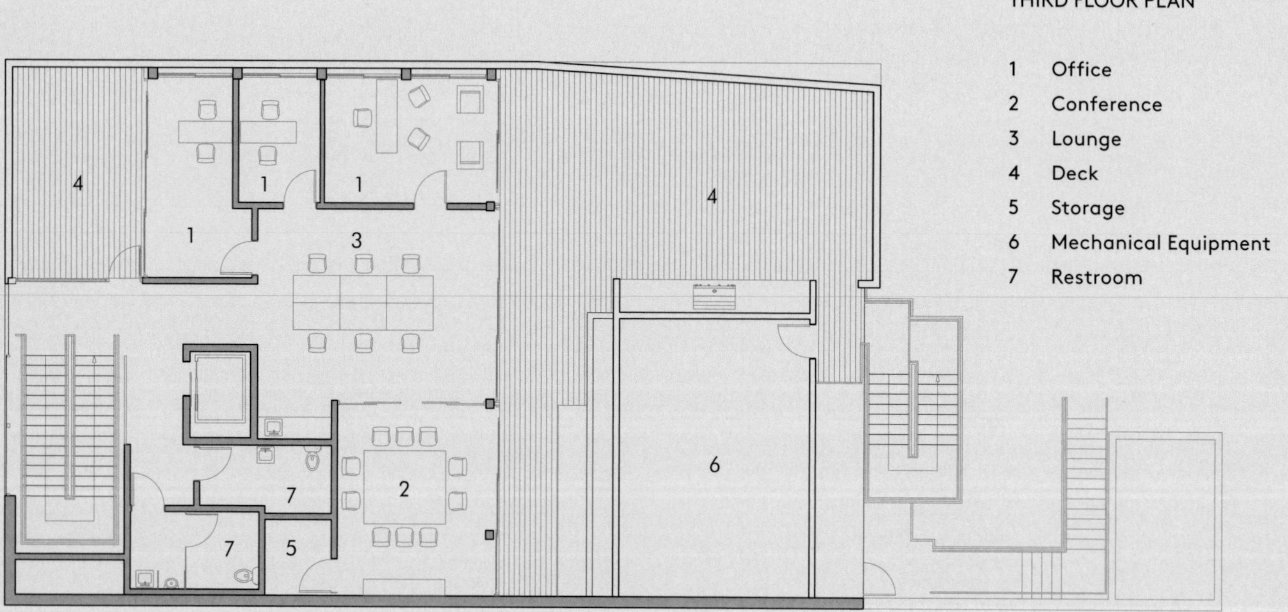

THE LABEL

Chicago Scoring Stage
Chicago, Illinois

Third Coast Music is an organization dedicated to resurrecting Chicago as a recording hub for the music industry. Two accomplished classical concert violinists have formed the group to develop the Chicago Studio Orchestra and to foster music for the growing film and television industry in the city.

Recognizing that there is no large scoring facility that can accommodate Chicago's growing postproduction needs, Third Coast is planning to build a new state-of-the-art scoring stage to attract the growing film and TV industry in the area and worldwide.

The studio will serve as a core for the artistic development in the city and create work and employment opportunities for local musicians. It will provide assets to colleges and universities for classes and seminars, internships and workshops.

The conceptual design consists of a scoring stage for at least one hundred musicians, complemented by choral and observation balconies and five different isolation booths. Control and mix rooms will also be built, along with the necessary infrastructure to run and service a major facility of this scale, such as edit bays, mastering rooms, and production offices.

Having a facility of this caliber in the city will help retain local musical and engineering talent who now often leave for cities like Los Angeles, New York, or Nashville.

The project is supported by the local musicians' unions, the Chicago Philharmonic and many arts and governmental organizations in the city. Third Coast will devlop and manage the scoring stage facility and is currently raising funds to make it a reality.

4 Enhance

Post Logic 1995

Asymmetrical 1997

Fox Audio 2017

FLOOR PLAN

1 Large Mix Bays
2 Small Mix Bays
3 Iso Booth/Mix Bay
4 Central Machine Room
5 Engineering
6 Headphone Stations
7 Media Administration
8 Office
9 Workstations
10 Lounge/Pantry
11 Electrical Room
12 Storage
13 Recorder Room
14 Amp Room

Record Plant SoBe 2003

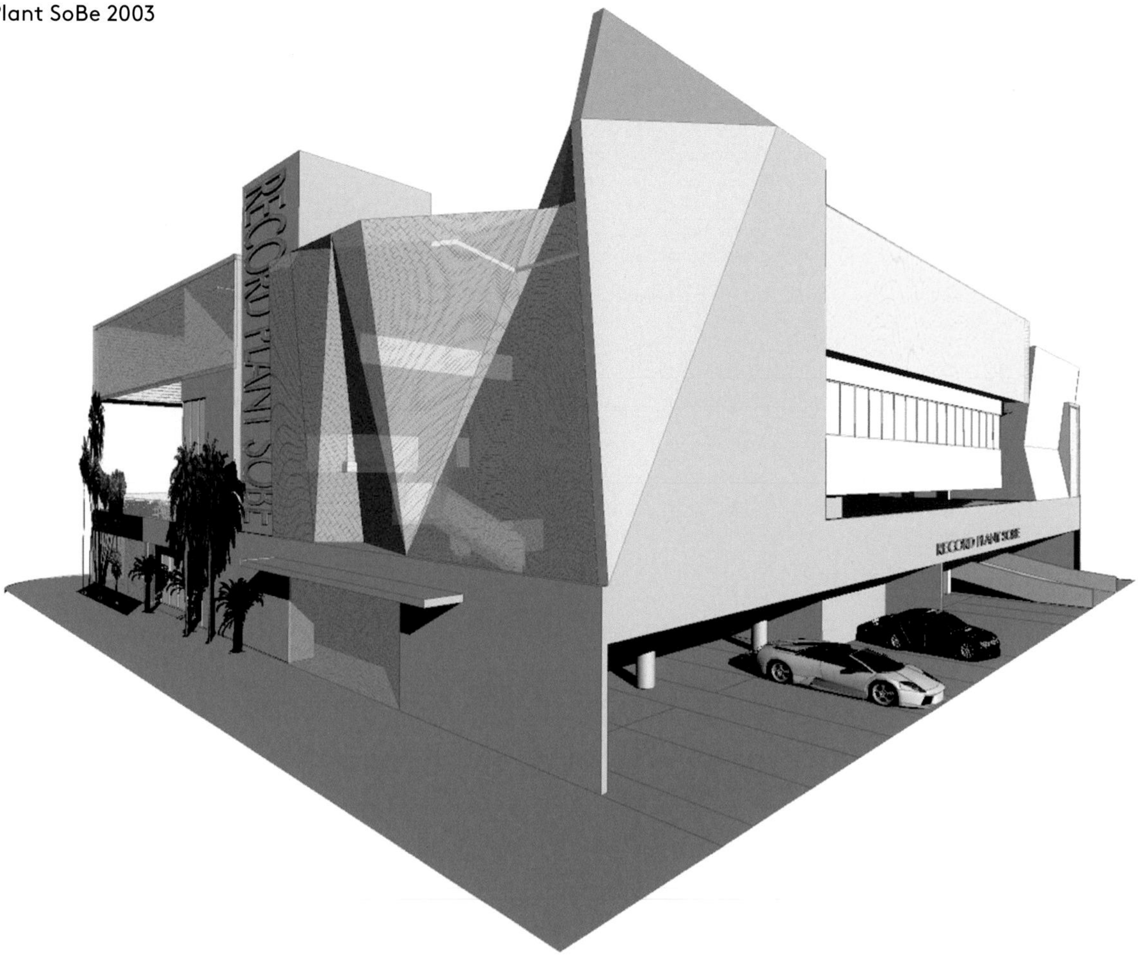

Audiophase 1999

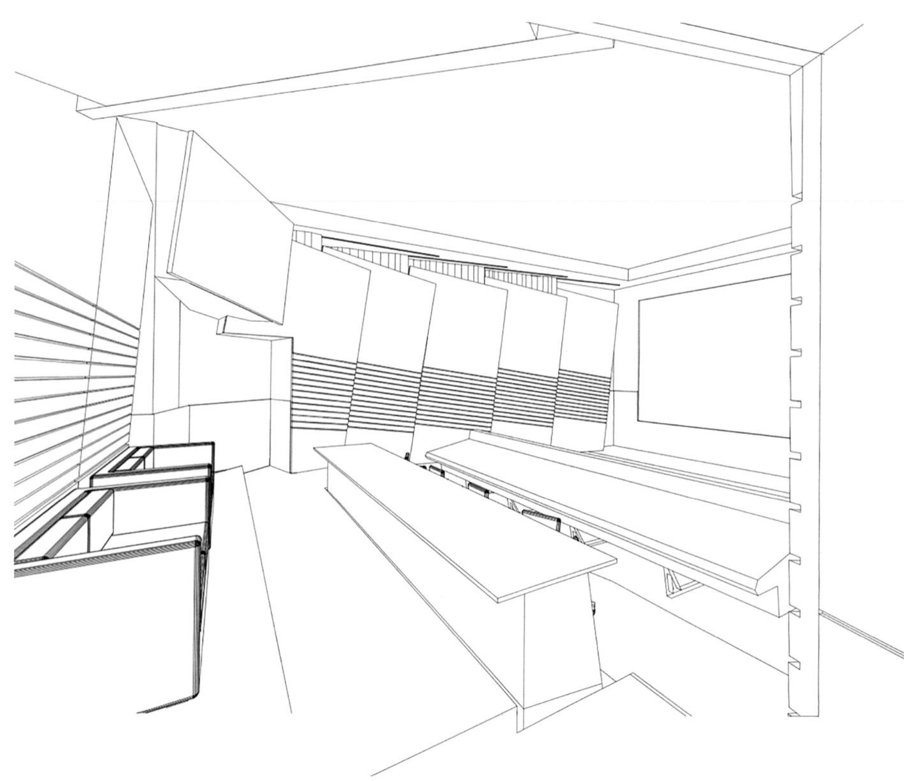

Dakota 2008

Conversation

Brian Riordan with David Goggin

DG The materials and design of this facility are very attractive. Is it for your comfort or for the client's comfort?

BR I have to say both. I certainly enjoy architecture and interior design and art. It was important to build a place that I wanted to come to every day. And we want something that clients are going to feel is both open and airy and light. By contrast, most of the facilities in the 70s and 80s had narrow hallways, low ceilings, and no windows. So, for us the goal was to find a building that had a nice ceiling span and had a lot of light. And then, in terms of the aesthetics, Peter really incorporated a lot of the work that was already here. There are a lot of clean straight lines; it's a building that was built in the late 40s and lends itself to minimalist, straight edge line design.

DG How long have you been doing this type of work?

BR I've been in this business since 1995, when I moved to LA. I was recording and producing my own music and other people's music in Boston, and when I came to LA, I got into audio for video games and commercials, award shows, and anything where live musicians were performing on television. I started my own company in 1999, up the street from here, and I bought this building in 2005. We were in construction for about fourteen months before we opened in 2006.

DG Your building has individually isolated studios for concentrating hard on the postproduction work, which has to sound great. But the actual atmosphere throughout seems to be very conducive to a pleasant workflow from one stage of the process to another. How much of your vision was creating this atmosphere?

BR It was very, very important to the process, making a place that was comfortable for clients who are typically working in dingy production offices. For them to come here, it's relaxing; it's sort of a de-stressor. We want people to walk in and immediately feel like this is a creative, professional environment, but it's not corporate stuffy, stressful, dramatic. That is achieved first by the physical structure of the place.

DG There's plenty of space here as contrasted with the concentrated workrooms where you're focusing on image and trying to create the sound that captures the action. It must be helpful to be able to step outside.

BR It is. Step outside, and you have natural light, something that studios don't have. You have a nice flow of air, and so the building itself and the interior design is one way you achieve that. The other is by the personnel. Having a staff that is warm, inviting, no ego, calming, professional, and hardworking is a never-ending effort. The building is maintained so that those two aspects come together. Hopefully, people get a sense of happiness and feel welcome. It's a combination of those two elements, the building and the people.

DG You've been in this business for more than twenty years, and the industry has gone from analog to digital. To satisfy your caliber of clientele, you always have to be on the cutting edge, which is risky. Things go in different directions; the requirements change. Did you have that in mind when you designed a facility that is able to accommodate whatever those changes may be? You continually need to pull gear out and put in some new gear. Has that been true?

BR It has been true. Fortunately, on the upside of things of where we are now versus where we were twenty-five years ago, the equipment itself has been minimized in terms of what you need in a room; we don't have any outboard gear other than mic preamps and compressors and only for recording. Mixing is 100 per cent in the box, so we're using all Avid design

Brian Riordan with Mr. Bonzai

consoles that essentially are giant remote controls for Pro Tools digital processing. Everything's streamlined from where it used to be, and that is also true with economics.

The days of having to buy a half-million-dollar console – which was happening in the music world back then – those days in post production are over. Today, you can spend a hundred grand and get a nice Avid S6 console. The downside for me is that all of my rooms have to be completely uniform for the way that we work. Every room has to have the exact same complement of gear. I have nine mix rooms and six edit bays in-house, and if I buy one of something for every room, that multiplies pretty quickly. Even just one little plug-in for 1500 bucks means that now I'm buying 15 of them. And that goes too with a projector or a console, so it's a volume game now.

DG Well, you seem to be comfortable today with all those changes coming down the road. Where do you see Levels Audio in five years?

BR Well, we just built our second Atmos bay at the end of last year. I do think that Dolby Atmos for home theater and broadcast is really taking shape to become a norm, but there's still 5.1 surround sound at home, and that is a considerably smaller percentage than those who just watch in stereo. But I do think it's going to become a much more day-to-day medium. Amazon and all the OTT companies – Netflix, Apple, Hulu – are going in that direction. Netflix requires it now, and everyone's trying to follow suit. And for us, we're on the front end of that; I think we'll end up five years from now having quite a few more Atmos bays. And right now we're almost tapeless, and tape is going away quickly.

DG This is a very competitive market, and you're in the entertainment capital of the world. Is it important for your company to have its own clear identity, a brand?

BR Absolutely. I feel that it's been critical to our success. We were branded – whether it was self-intentional or not – but we were known for many years as a luxury post production brand in the work that we do. Whereas we're more expensive, a little higher end, you get a little better quality, but you have to pay for it. And sometimes that would work against us, where we would bid against projects and lose out. But when the business and the industry and the economy are ebbing and flowing, I feel like those luxury brands hold on. Neiman Marcus and Saks Fifth Avenue – I don't think they were struggling. They were holding on. A certain percentage of their clients were going to go, regardless. I think Sears and JC Penney probably had a way harder time when things were going down like that.

DG You're not only the owner. You're actively doing what all the other engineers here are doing. Is it important to convey to your clientele that you're actually here, you're hands on, and you have to make all of it work for yourself?

BR It's incredibly important, but I think it happened in reverse order. I started as a one-man band getting clients, and then the goal was to get them to work with other people. Staying actively involved, still to this day, is completely critical. There's a sense of client comfort, and while I may not be the one mixing their show, they know that I'm involved. They know that I'm working with the mixer directly here, sitting in the room with them during a spotting session, or during their review, and they know that they can call my cell phone at three o'clock in the morning on any night of the week if there's a real emergency, and that I'll pick up and handle it.

I also think that it's equally as important to my team of mixers and editors to know that I'm in the trenches with them. It creates a level of trust, and they work even harder because they respect that.

DG In the evolution of your business, is there a continuing dialogue with Peter as you expand and refine this workplace?

BR Peter is always my go-to guy, whether he likes it or not. I get a lot of wild ideas in the middle of the night, and sometimes I get talked out of them by the people around me, for good reasons, but sometimes we go, "Yeah, it sounds like a good idea." And this building specifically has been in design and construction since we did the full build-out and opened the summer of '06. Every two years or so, Peter continues working with us, whether it's small or large.

We always seem to be working on design projects. His talent is to see the large picture and all the internal flow. If we add this, we've got to think about how this affects this, and how that affects that. He can tie it in, pushing the building back and having that feel and look so that ultimately it's new, but it has this amazing flow, where it just seems as if it's always existed.

Brian Riordan is an audio mixer and entrepreneur. He owns Levels Audio and is the founder of the Hollywood Compassion Coalition.

Levels
Hollywood, California

After a long search, a former movie equipment rental store and warehouse with long bow-truss spans was chosen as the relocation site for Levels Audio, a production facility for television, movies, and multimedia sound. The move from a smaller scale Art Deco building to the 14,000-square-foot raw building shell presented an opportunity to build updated studios, as well as generous, yet intimate lounges for client and staff interaction.

The design and construction did not come without challenges. A strongly sloping main floor was only discovered after the labyrinthine build-out on both floors had been removed, and along with difficult access to the basement and noise from the street, it became one of the challenges posed by the new location.

The design parti utilizes the large open space to the fullest extent and maintains the character of the old industrial shell by keeping it exposed where possible. For economy and sustainability, as little as possible of the building envelope was changed, and the insertion of the various new elements was kept suggestive of the remaining old parts.

The ground floor is organized with a dense row of four studio suites along the northern wall, leaving the south side free for open space and access from the adjacent parking lot. An aluminum-clad lounge and office is suspended above the reception, overlooking the open volume. The basement houses smaller studios, affiliated video editing and special effects companies, and a central machine room. A new large cut in the floor permitted the insertion of a relocated new central staircase and allows daylight to reach the lower level lounge and connects it to the main floor.

Since there is almost no visitor foot traffic, the main entrance was relocated to the side of the building, adjacent to the parking lot. It is framed by a new volume of metal walls and roofs, marking the new access point. Transformers and other electrical equipment are concealed behind the corrugated steel panels, helping to add depth to the entrance.

The light-filled space of the main lounge, with its skylights, brick and concrete walls, wood slats, and concrete floors, offers a relaxing contrast to the concentrated and intense atmosphere inside the studios. Inspired by the owner's family connection with a lumber company, the recurring theme of the space and the exterior of the building is a system of horizontal cedar slats, complemented by long narrow light tubes.

Identical common materials are used inside and out; wood slats, polycarbonate panels, and corrugated aluminum and galvanized steel occur throughout the building. Arranged in shades of blue and white, the recurring horizontal lights on the exterior relate to the traffic flow on Highland Avenue but are also faintly reminiscent of sound level meters, the image behind the company name. Inside, the same lights alternate with video screens, and continue suspended below the open roof, framing an abstract rectangular volume within the building shell.

Besides fabric wall coverings, environmentally friendly cotton is used for sound absorption in the studio spaces, adding to the natural feel of the wood strips. Floors are polished concrete, covered in concrete topping or carpet when required by the acoustics.

A system of ramps and platforms helps overcome the eighteen-inch difference in height between the back and the front of the building, but also serves to access the raised and floating acoustic separation floors inside all of the studios. The main problem in the basement is the limited ceiling height, but due to the need for more space, several new studio suites have been added there over time.

The final addition, now maximizing every available square foot, was the construction of one more studio suite in 2017. It has replaced what was previously the largest room as the flagship space of the facility and is equipped with the latest surround sound technology, an increasingly common requirement from content providers.

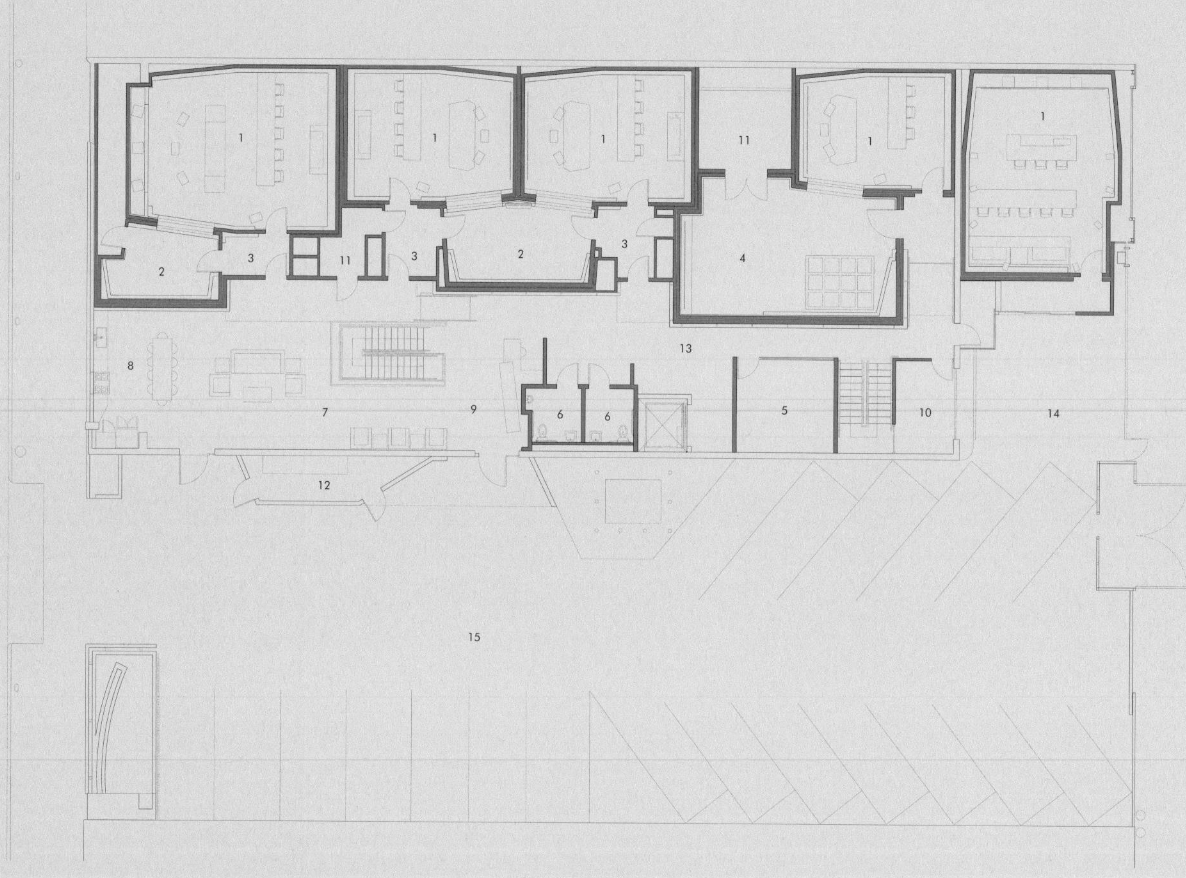

GROUND FLOOR PLAN

1 Mix Room
2 Voice-over booth
3 Sound Lock
4 Foley / ADR Studio
5 Studio Manager
6 Bathroom
7 Lounge
8 Kitchen
9 Reception
10 Office
11 Storage
12 Utilities
13 Hallway
14 Loading Dock
15 Parking Lot

RUNNIN' DOWN A DREAM
TOM PETTY
AND THE HEARTBREAKERS
DELL

EXIT

1026

LEVELS
1026

LEVELS
audio
EXIT

LEVELS
audio

Farm Group LA
Hollywood, California

After taking over an existing video editing firm, the London-based Farm Group expanded its LA home by adding a new audio postproduction facility in an adjacent empty space. By constructing new studios in a vacant portion of the building, as well as improving support spaces, it doubled the total size of the original footprint to 6,000 square feet. The work of the firm, much like in its existing studios in the UK, is geared heavily towards music-oriented TV shows, such as reality television competitions.

The construction had to take place within and next to a fully functioning studio facility, posing serious scheduling and coordination challenges. Even more importantly, reconfiguring and relocating the technical infrastructure for both the existing and the new studios required a very delicate operation. The new shared central machine room is now servicing both the video and audio components of the whole facility. Two identical television sound mixing rooms make up most of the remainder of the expansion. A shared voice-over booth between them can be used by either room while being closed off with privacy curtains from the other.

To achieve a clean and modern aesthetic, simple boxes with white walls were inserted into the industrial bow-truss building and visually connected with polished concrete floors. The warm feel of the raw wood roof structure in the open common areas contrasts with the new build-out, which is lit by generous and newly restored skylights. To maintain the light and airy feeling of the daylit volumes, a new sound lock space was built entirely of glass and positioned just below a skylight.

The look of the more secluded production spaces loosely evolved from the company's studios in the UK, but was customized with the use of computer-controlled milling. The laser-cut white wall panels in the studios fulfill both a visual and acoustical purpose. To generate the patterns, the farm-themed animal logos of the firm were pixelated and enlarged. They were then positioned to match the acoustic requirements of each wall. For further acoustic control, some of the panels were slightly tilted from the vertical plane. The pattern is still somewhat evocative of the original animals but provides an abstracted image for visual interest, without distracting from the images and sound being processed. Interestingly, even after years in the studios, many users are unaware of the origin of the patterns.

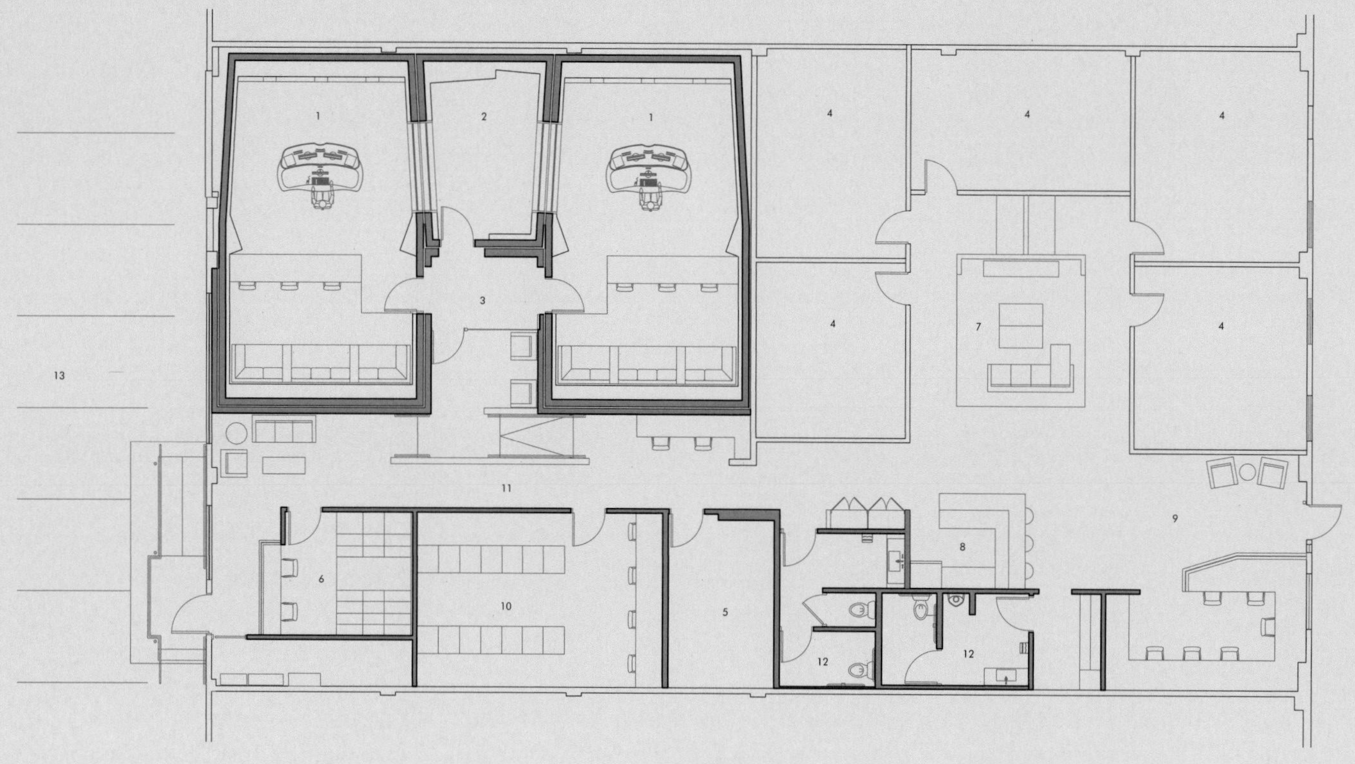

FLOOR PLAN

1 Mix Room
2 Voice-over booth
3 Sound Lock
4 Edit Bay
5 Meeting Room
6 Archives
7 Lounge
8 Kitchen
9 Lobby
10 Equipment Room
11 Hallway
12 Restroom
13 Parking

Company logos converted to acoustic panels

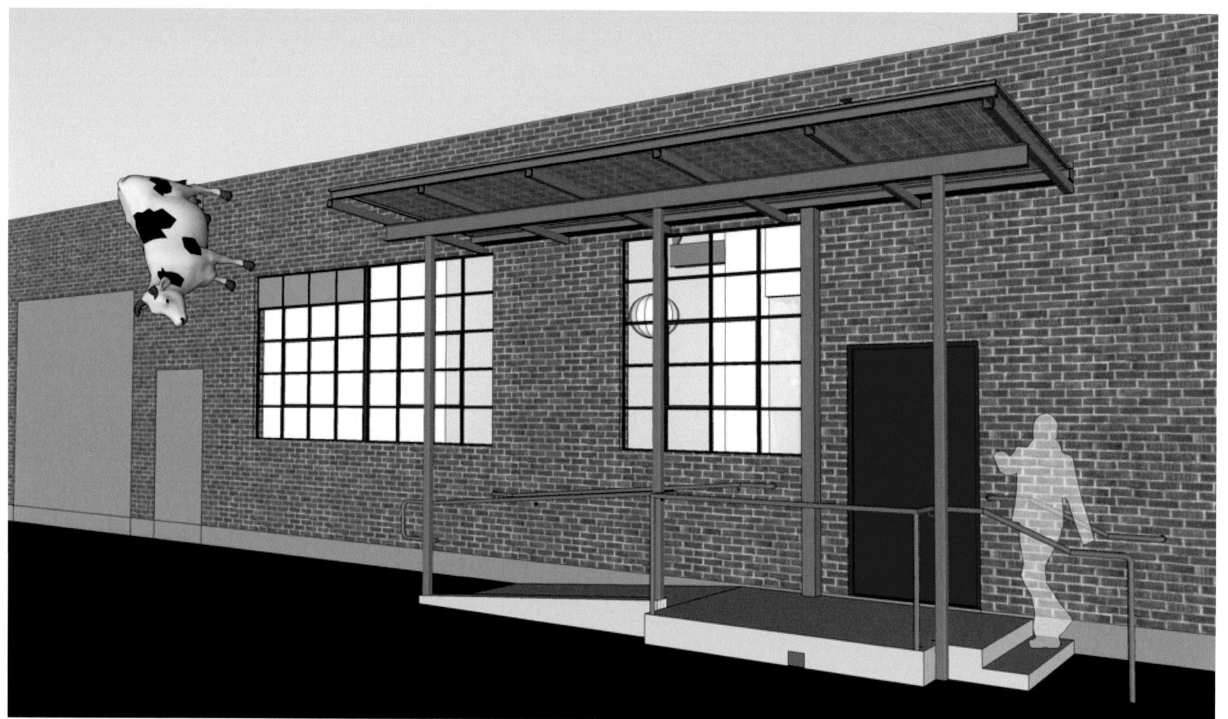

Proposed signage

Shochiku MediaWorx

Tokyo, Japan

The 18,000-square-foot project is situated on two full floors of a contemporary office tower on Tokyo Bay. The program includes music recording, ADR/Foley and postproduction studios for audio and video, a dubbing stage, and office space. The taller floor height on the ground floor was ideal for the dubbing stage and more public functions, while the smaller spaces are located on a floor higher up in the building.

The design approach considers the broad and varied range of activities and the historic span of artistic enterprises undertaken by the Shochiku Corporation and Shochiku MediaWorx in particular. That history includes the continuity of its cultural endeavors, from the nurturing of traditional Kabuki theater and the restoration and preservation work on historic Japanese movies to the production of contemporary motion pictures.

A nostalgic or pseudotraditional environment for the studios was not appropriate, but a typical, standard, corporate environment was not desirable either. While searching for a more customized approach that would reflect the history as well as the present and the future of the company, designing a functional and highly efficient facility always remained a high priority. One point of departure and the main inspiration for the wall surfaces in the studios are the slatted wood walls, screens, and panels found in traditional Japanese architecture. Another element used throughout the project is a rectangle with a two to one ratio, a common shape, as seen for example in tatami mats. The traditionally proportioned panels are then divided diagonally to arrive at two triangles. Rendered in wood and fabric-covered panels as well as translucent plexiglass, the shapes are sometimes slanted and recur in both the studios and the general areas of the project.

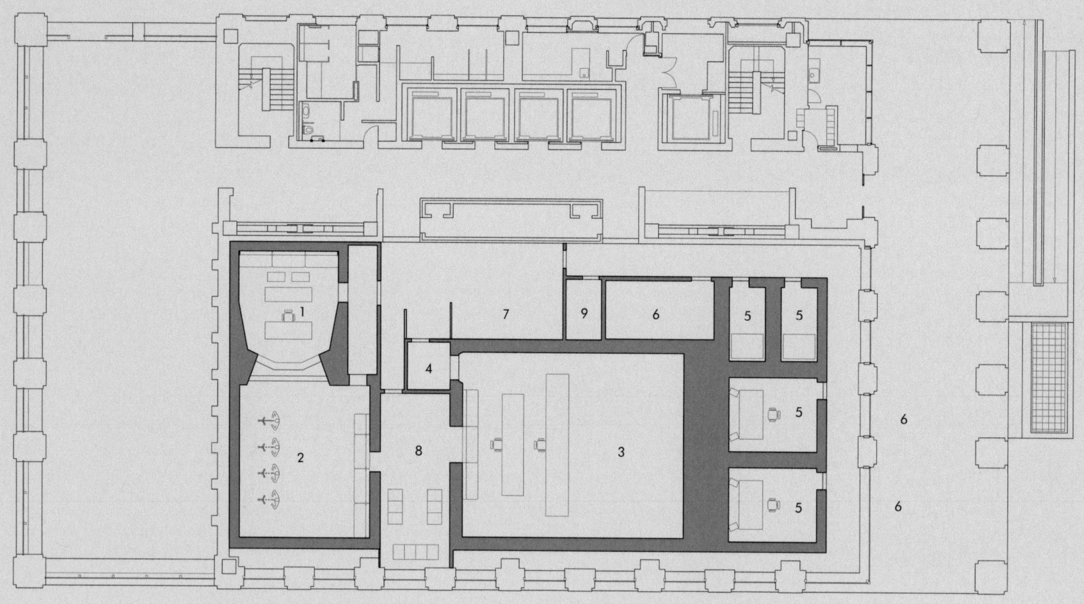

GROUND FLOOR PLAN

1 ADR Control Room
2 ADR
3 Dubbing Stage
4 Sound Lock
5 Sound Design
6 Editing Room
7 Lobby
8 Machine Room
9 Storage

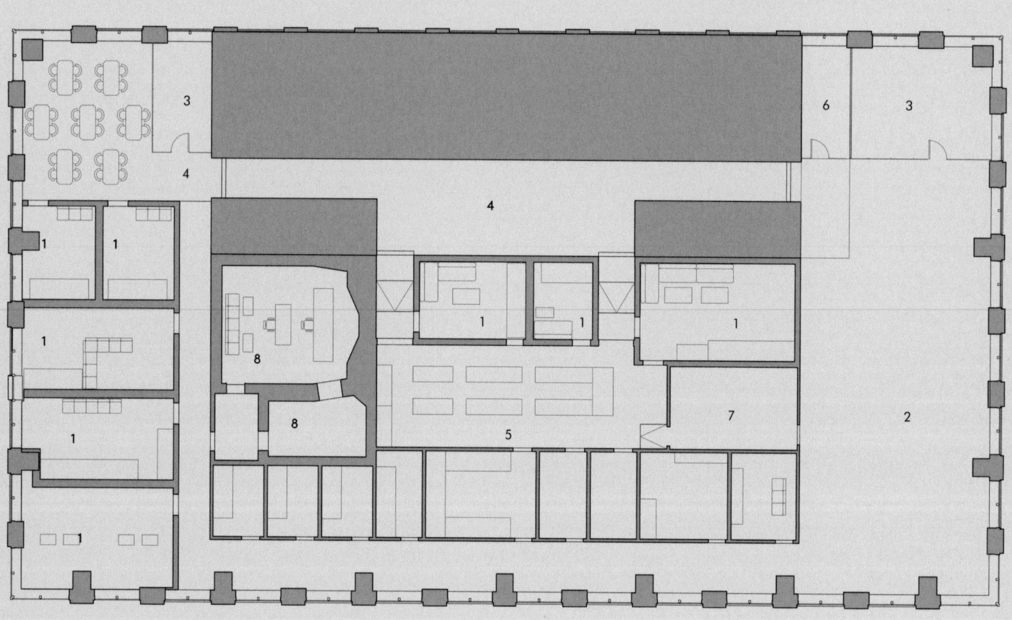

UPPER FLOOR PLAN

1 Editing Room
2 Office
3 Meeting Room
4 Lobby
5 Machine Room
6 Equipment Room
7 Storage
8 Audio Suite

740 Sound

Playa del Rey, California

While many Los Angeles area sound facilities are located in Hollywood, the San Fernando Valley, Santa Monica, and Culver City, several advertising agencies are concentrated in the Playa del Rey neighborhood. Creating sound for advertising is one of the main trades of 740 Sound Design, a company owned by a sound designer and executive producer. Its aim is to provide feature-film-quality sound design for commercials. So it was a logical next step to put the new home for the company there, just ahead of the current rush of tech companies taking over millions of square feet of creative space in the area.

The warehouse chosen for the project previously housed many of Frank Gehry's architectural models, next door to his own office. The relocated project now also includes 740's audio postproduction facility, allowing it to add mixing to its sound design service. Ten times larger than the company's previous space, the facility includes two mixing stages, two voice-over/Foley rooms, and multiple sound design rooms. The streamlined mixing suites and edit bays take up about two-thirds of the 9,000-square-foot facility, leaving room to build additional studios in the future.

That vacant open space was utilized to place a generously sized open kitchen and lounge area at the core of the new design. A central table island is used for gatherings and to lay out food. It still leaves plenty of remaining space to relax and mingle or play a game of ping pong. The east-facing old industrial roll-up door at the front was replaced by a glazed overhead door.

In the studio area, a sky lit sound lock and vestibule lead into the large mix rooms and the recording spaces, the larger of which, at over 300 square feet, can accommodate Foley, ADR, music recording, and more. The mix rooms feature built-in workstations and large client desks and are connected to a central machine room. Wood tones and fabric surfaces are balanced with natural concrete floors and crisp and clean detailing, offering a focused yet relaxed work environment. Indirect lighting is added besides the ceiling can task lights, and custom-designed wood furniture is kept very simple and straightforward.

Several smaller interior additions, such as a second vocal booth, additional edit rooms and offices were added after the initial build-out.

GROUND FLOOR PLAN

1 Mix Room
2 Isolation Booth
3 Sound Lock
4 Kitchenette
5 Machine Room
6 Electrical Room
7 Bathroom

5 Share

47
AMERICAN FEDERATION
OF MUSICIANS
REHEARSAL HALL

npr

Art Institute 2008

SM Airport Park 2017

YG Proposal 2015

Stade de Suisse 2003

CRA 2003

Conversation
Craig Hodgetts with Michael Webb

MW Do all notable buildings have the potential of a second life that will bring them into the public realm?

CH Yes, if there is a powerful organization to manage, program, and maintain them. It's a critical part of the equation. Bricks and mortar aren't enough. You can restore the glorious theaters on Broadway downtown, and people can come and admire them, but without programming they will stay dead.

MW Are there general principles that apply to every rejuvenation or adaptive re-use project?

CH What you have to do is consider the needs of a contemporary audience and find a way of marrying their expectations for a theatrical or musical performance with the potential of the venue. For instance, the Egyptian Theater [a 1922 movie palace on Hollywood Boulevard] had a postage-stamp screen prior to Michael Todd coming with his extravaganza *Around the World in 80 Days* and leaving a trail of destruction. We tried to preserve its character while adapting it to the needs of the American Cinematheque, making it a fantastic place to see a movie.

We left the original décor intact and inserted two new auditoria into the old to have a comfortable and inaudible air-conditioning system, good acoustics and sightlines, as well as a manageable number of seats. We moved the screen to the back of the stage and built an acoustical box behind that. Some historians were upset by what we did, but you have to balance their concerns with that of the audience.

MW You reconstructed the Hollywood Bowl after earlier schemes of improvement had fallen short, including one by Frank Gehry. That must have been challenging and even more controversial.

CH The Hollywood Bowl has been an icon since the 1920s so people were very attached to what was there. Its seating and the character were givens. But the shell was a disaster for the orchestra and that motivated the entire reconstruction. The musicians felt incapable of performing as an ensemble because they couldn't hear each other play. Ernest Fleischmann, the manager of the LA Philharmonic, wanted to bring in a new conductor, but the contenders said they couldn't perform there. The old shell was constructed from asbestos cement and was decaying. There was also the economic driver: the Philharmonic use it for summer concerts of classical music, but it's also leased for pop concerts, and we had to consider how long it took to install the lighting and speakers for those events. In two years of studies, we considered what could be done with the existing shell, using all kinds of stratagems, but we finally concluded that a new structure was needed.

We enlarged the shell to accommodate the entire orchestra under the reflecting surface and to ensure there was no feedback from the speakers. It was pure geometry, and you had to accept the form that came out of it. The parameters were inexorable. There's a flat plane over the orchestra to reflect the sound back to the players; for the audience, the sound is amplified as it has been for decades. The speakers remain where they were even though they still partially block the audience's view of the shell.

MW Most recently you upgraded the Robert Frost high school auditorium to remedy its deficiencies and enhance its qualities. How did you approach that job?

CH Our mission was to make it a vibrant performing arts center. Culver City High prepares students for careers in production and stagecraft, but the first priority of the school board was the poor air quality and the health of the users. So, after a forensic study of the entire facility, we discovered that the air was coming from the side walls and not reaching the center of the auditorium or the stage. The answer was to bring in air from smaller units in the ceiling, and to combine it with improvements in the acoustics and lighting. The concrete roof vault was too thin to accept heavier loads, so we introduced a steel arch over the stage from which to suspend the new equipment. Everything was driven by function not cosmetics. The project was underway before the client realized that the theater could be rented out to generate revenue, and so we enlarged the ticket booth and made other improvements.

MW What lessons have you learned from those three projects and how widely applicable are they?

CH Philanthropists and affluent patrons provide a support framework for prestigious performing arts centers. Our projects are black sheep and have had to support themselves. For example, we were rebuilding the Hollywood Bowl at the same time as Disney Hall was being erected, and that was getting all the attention. The Bowl is run by the LA County Department of Parks and Recreation and doesn't have the same prestige. So we focused on the popular audience, not the elite, and that was very rewarding.

MW Beyond technical and physical changes, what other factors impact performance and atmosphere?

CH At the Frost, we realized the lobby was too confined, so we created a courtyard where the audience could gather before a performance – an important part of the experience. It was the same at the Egyptian, where the linear courtyard leading off the street was a bare expanse. We had a long wrestling match with the historical people when we insisted on planting palm trees and installing seating where you can linger over a drink. That outdoor space is rented out for parties and events, and is used as often as the theaters it serves. One of the big disappointments at the Bowl was that nobody understood our plan for a dramatic front entry with lighting and a canopy where people could socialize and build anticipation for the performance. It's still relegated to parking.

MW: When working on tight budgets, can small moves have a big impact?

CH Before the Bowl we were working with a couple of movie chains to revamp their theaters. We organized focus groups to determine audience preferences. The seat was their first concern, followed by the sound and the concessions; the quality of the picture was never mentioned. We selected an inexpensive seat that was fabricated in Mexico, and the response was highly favorable.

MW You've spoken of things that are within and beyond the designer's reach. Can you elucidate?

CH One of the reasons our work in this field has been successful is that we have a lot of empathy for the players and the audience. When we were designing the new Nashville amphitheater, we insisted on superior backstage facilities. If you want to get a great performance, it's essential to provide comfortable spaces in which the performers can relax and unwind. You have to bring sincerity and enthusiasm to projects like these. That's what makes it such an exciting design opportunity. There are so many factors to consider, and it's not just a question of money but paying careful attention to every aspect and creating a harmonious whole.

Craig Hodgetts is a design partner, along with Ming Fung, at Mithun/Hodgetts+Fung and professor emeritus of the UCLA architectural faculty. He is known for his imaginative designs and writing and has created public projects such as the Hollywood Bowl reconstruction and the Egyptian Theater remodel.

Essay

Music Spaces in Berlin and Los Angeles

There are surprising parallels between the sister cities of Berlin and Los Angeles, as is convincingly shown in the Getty exhibition *Berlin/Los Angeles: Space for Music* – kinships not only in urban development but also in the arts and philosophical outlook. A common thread persists below the surface of the obvious differences in their histories.[1]

By comparing two of the most iconic structures built for music performance over the last century, the exhibition at the Getty Research Institute illustrates some of the two cities' commonalities in a new and revealing way. The juxtaposition of Hans Scharoun's 1963 Philharmonic in Berlin and Frank Gehry's 2003 Disney Hall in LA brings to light strong similarities from architectural, acoustical, and musical, as well as social and urban, points of view.

Spaces for Music

Both projects can be seen as the culmination of each architect's development toward a perfect space for musical performance. Hans Scharoun had designed and built theaters before, incorporating elements that would reach their ultimate expression in the concert hall for the Berlin Philharmonic. During the decade-long delay before construction began on Disney Hall, Frank Gehry had the opportunity to design the Guggenheim Museum in Bilbao. The formal language and expressive power of that project translated seamlessly to the Los Angeles concert hall.

Sketches and models by Scharoun and Gehry, as well as photographs of the two buildings, show a clear lineage between the two structures and their architects. To see a 1940s Scharoun watercolor sketch directly above a 2012 photograph of Disney Hall is a revelation. Further proof of a close connection is easy to find throughout the exhibition in drawings and writings about the architecture but also in the relationship of these firm yet fluid structures with their intended use as vessels dedicated to music.

Gehry's question, "If architecture is frozen music, is music liquid architecture?" and Scharoun's statement, "Music should be at the center, spatially as well as visually," sum up many of the ideas behind the two buildings.

Scharoun continues: "Here the creation and the experience of music occur in a hall not motivated by formal aesthetics, but whose design was inspired by the very purpose it serves."[2] Although his exuberant expressionism was something of an outlier within the orthodoxy of the time, Scharoun's design, completed at the height of the modern movement, is a pure expression of the shape of the main auditorium, with even the smallest ancillary space being greatly influenced by it. There are no shortcuts; the architectural form is determined by its function, artistically, acoustically, and socially.

Disney Hall, designed about thirty years later, is freer in its approach. The exterior does not literally represent the auditorium, and acoustically the hall is more of a hybrid between the revolutionary vineyard concept Scharoun perfected, with terraced seating around the orchestra at center, and the shoebox shape of more traditional halls.

The exhibition traces architectural history up to the present by spotlighting another concert hall by Frank Gehry, the newly completed Pierre Boulez Hall in Berlin. Another hybrid, this project places a smaller vineyard-type auditorium inside a rectangular box, all within an existing historic building, reminiscent of Gehry's DZ Bank building in Pariser Platz just down the street.

Walt Disney Concert Hall, Los Angeles

The inclusion of the Pierre Boulez Hall highlights the affinity between the two architectural main acts and reinforces the social agenda espoused by both Scharoun and Gehry. Serving the Barenboim-Said Academy, an institution that is meant to bring together Palestinian and Israeli musicians, the new Boulez Hall signifies much more than just a space for music.

Elite Utopianism

A democratic, humanitarian, and utopian approach was at the core of Scharoun's work. He meant to design buildings for all people – not just the elite few. Similarly, Gehry's interpretation of donor Lillian B. Disney's wish for a garden resulted in a new public open space, and his insistence on allowing the public to walk up and around the hall has enriched the urban landscape around Disney Hall.

The dedication of Gehry's newest Berlin project to Pierre Boulez, a giant of modern classical music, is fitting as well. Scharoun's Philharmonic was meant as an experimental space, trying out new audience and stage configurations, and even orchestral arrangements, in the service of the music and its performance and experience. Likewise, Disney Hall is designed for new and contemporary music as much as for a traditional classical repertoire. Music director Esa-Pekka Salonen helps reinforce that mission, and the inclusionary approach fostered by his successor Gustavo Dudamel further expands its social relevance.

New Spaces for Music

Despite these progressive ideals, all three projects still represent the epitome of elite culture, rarefied structures in a chaotic world. The concert halls represent a visionary ideal, but in both Berlin and LA countless other spaces for music exist in many other forms – more improvised, nontraditional, and open-ended, sometimes even scrappy and run-down.

Both metropolises are creative centers of film, home to the oldest large film studio in existence, Babelsberg Studio outside Berlin, and to the large-scale entertainment production complex known as Hollywood in and around Los Angeles. Film and music being closely related, the highly accomplished musicians in both cities often work on movie scores, in closed scoring stages, studio spaces, and production facilities. Away from the public eye, music is made in a multitude of different spaces.

Berliner Philharmonie, Architekt Hans Scharoun

Studios for recording and music production complement a vibrant live music scene in both places. David Bowie was a legendary musical visitor to Berlin, where he recorded some of his most creative albums. He recalls a story told by his friend Iggy Pop, who had been out late at a punk club on the anniversary of the Berlin Wall's construction. A replica of the wall had been put up in the basement club and was then viciously torn down by the patrons. After the riot, in an affecting scene, the hardened punks sat down, exhausted, with tears streaming down their faces. Music, world politics, the sadness of the divided city, the revolt of the disenfranchised and architecture were all coming together in that basement space.[3]

Like the teenage addict protagonist in the movie, *We Children from Bahnhof Zoo*[4], who looks forward to Bowie's concert, people in all circumstances are inspired and moved by music. The sound and the spaces in which it is made offer a temporary escape from sometimes – harsh reality.

Both Berlin and LA provide endless spatial opportunities for the making and production of music. The decommissioned factories used for techno dance parties in Berlin, the rock 'n roll clubs along Sunset Strip, the thousands of garage and home studios in LA, the basement jazz clubs, the rap venues in South LA, the open air festival grounds, the piers and squares and stadiums are all part of a landscape of spaces for music that is less pristine and sophisticated but maybe even more democratic than the shining temples of the concert hall.

While the three extraordinary projects featured in *Space for Music* represent the pinnacle of architecture and space for music and culture, they are just the tip of the proverbial iceberg.

1. Marissa Clifford and Emily Pugh, *Berlin/LA: Spaces for Music*, architecture and film, 2017, Getty Research Institute, Los Angeles, CA.
2. Peter Blundell Jones, *Hans Scharoun*, London: Phaidon Press, 1995, 35–36.
3. David Bowie, *VH1 Storytellers*, 1999, "We Children from Bahnhof Zoo (*Christiane F. - Wir Kinder vom Bahnhof Zoo*)," RCA Victor, 1981.
4. Directed by Uli Edel; Soundtrack by David Bowie.

A version of this essay was originally published in the Getty Iris Blog, Getty Research Institute, July 11, 2017, as *Berlin/ Los Angeles – Space for Music*. "Hitting the High Notes: Three Buildings by Two Architects" by Peter Grueneisen.

February 2017 © Volker Kreidler

Pierre Boulez Saal, Berlin

American Legion
Hollywood, California

The home of the American Legion Hollywood is a familiar sight on Highland Avenue near the Hollywood Bowl in Los Angeles. The original Art Deco building, a Los Angeles Historic-Cultural Monument since 1989, was initially conceived by World War One veterans as a clubhouse. It was designed by architects Weston and Weston and built in 1929 with in situ concrete, mostly by volunteer members themselves.

The clubhouse had been neglected over the years and featured impromptu additions and modifications. Besides the activities of the Legion Post, it housed an interactive play and stood in as a filming location for countless movies and TV shows.

The Post, due to its prominent location in the center of Hollywood's entertainment district and its local membership, has always been closely linked to the movie and entertainment world. The members have included prominent movie stars, performers, and musicians. A group of younger veterans recently decided to revive and again empower the building to its full potential. A theater committee was formed with the purpose of renovating the building for a new generation and tapping into the growing local need for performance venues and screening spaces.

The brief resulting from these efforts was a major renovation of the existing main meeting hall. With the revenue from the new theater, the non profit organization would be able to continue its mission to serve its members and to support veterans in need. The specific objective of the remodel was to convert the original multipurpose space and clubhouse into a state-of-the-art and high-end movie theater, suitable for exclusive events such as special screenings, premieres, and other happenings related to the booming Hollywood film industry.

To offer an attractive venue for movie presentations, the characteristics of the hall had to be adjusted, and some of its multipurpose aspects had to be slightly compromised. Nonetheless, flexibility in the use of the space was maintained, and lectures and live music or theater performances are still possible.

The refurbished space is a blend of the historic architectural character of the hall and its new contemporary build-out, still meant to reflect the dramatic flair reminiscent of old Hollywood movie palaces. The environment was designed to feel luxurious and fitting for a special event, in addition to providing excellent sound and pictures. The design builds upon and reinforces the unique architecture of the historic concrete building while providing technical and acoustic improvements and an environment suitable for today's needs and sensibilities.

By removing sideways facing risers and reshaping the floor with a slight rake, almost 500 seats, some of them removable to maintain a dance floor, were arranged in a newly curved continental arrangement. The rear risers were maintained but raised floor levels and ramped areas were introduced to facilitate diasabled access.

The sonic environment was improved with the use of surface treatments. The added absorption has lowered the reverberation time to less than half its original duration across a wide frequency range and is now balanced for movie projections. To generate the sound in the newly optimized space, a powerful audio system delivers one of the most exhilarating movie experiences anywhere. For the visual component, a new thirty-eight-foot wide screen, masking system and curtain, emphasized with uplighting from the stage floor, was installed.

Other building elements in particular need of improvement were the dilapidated and inoperable heating and cooling systems. Reversing the airflow and building a large soundproof air supply plenum in the banquet hall below the theater greatly improved the climate control. It also allowed for a new ceiling design with improved acoustics and looks in that basement space, known as the Cabaret Room.

In order to return the main space back to its original glory, decades of applied paint were removed, using a soda-blasting process and stripping the existing concrete to its natural state. Previously bare plaster walls were covered in acoustic fabric wedges, and a surround sound speaker system was integrated into the walls. Raw steel plates complement the roughness of the concrete and mediate between the fabric and wood finishes, waiting to acquire a rich patina over time.

The lower walls of the auditorium are now clad in perforated wood panels, patterned for acoustic purposes with pixelated and abstracted images from classic war movie scenes, thus bringing together the world of movies and the veterans' own experiences. The cutout pattern serves as a visual as well as a sound-absorbing element. The deep red fabric panels, seats, and carpet and the prominently placed gold concrete grilles add a more refined touch to the raw concrete and steel elements.

The addition of a disabled access lift to the side of the building cleared up the traffic flow into the building and to the auditorium, and a cantilevered bridge now leads to the original front doors of the clubhouse. The addition of the lift presented the opportunity to bring the front steps and the entrance up to code and to build wider steps and platforms for a better front approach. An added benefit was the improved appeal of the building's front as a central outdoor event space.

A new marquee and canopy over the entrance will offer future visitors a true red-carpet-arrival experience. It has been approved by the LA Office of Historic Resources, which has jurisdiction over the protected structure. For now, it remains incomplete, awaiting further fundraising efforts. But that did not prevent the Legion from hosting screenings for the annual Turner Classic Film Festival as the the main inaugural event for the new theater.

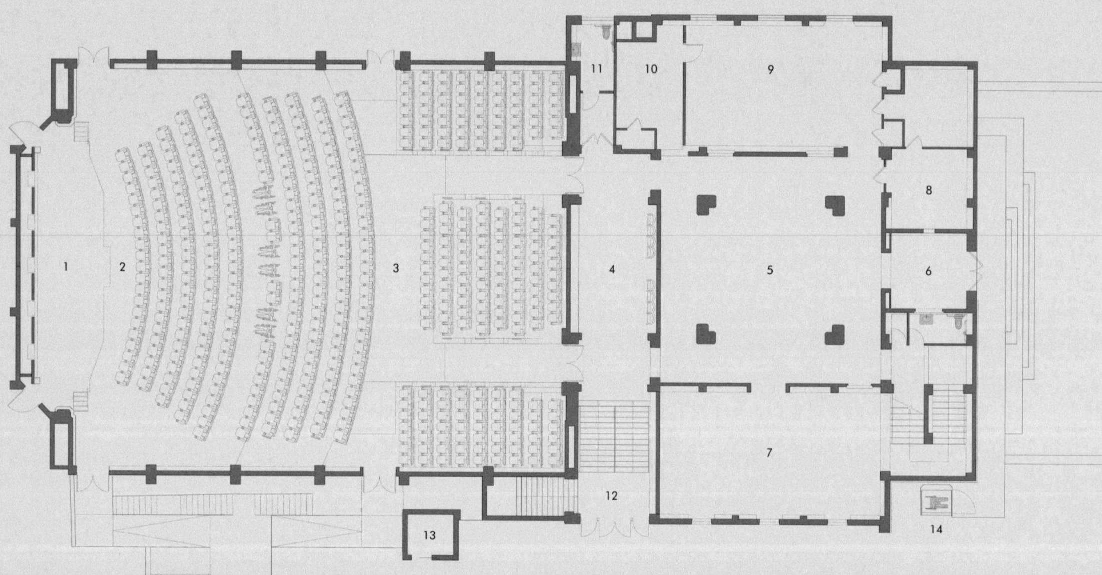

GROUND FLOOR PLAN

1 Stage and Screen
2 Removable Seating
3 Theater
4 Foyer
5 Rotunda
6 Vestibule
7 Trophy Room
8 Check Room
9 Event Room
10 Pantry
11 Restroom
12 Theater Entrance
13 Elevator
14 Disabled Access Lift

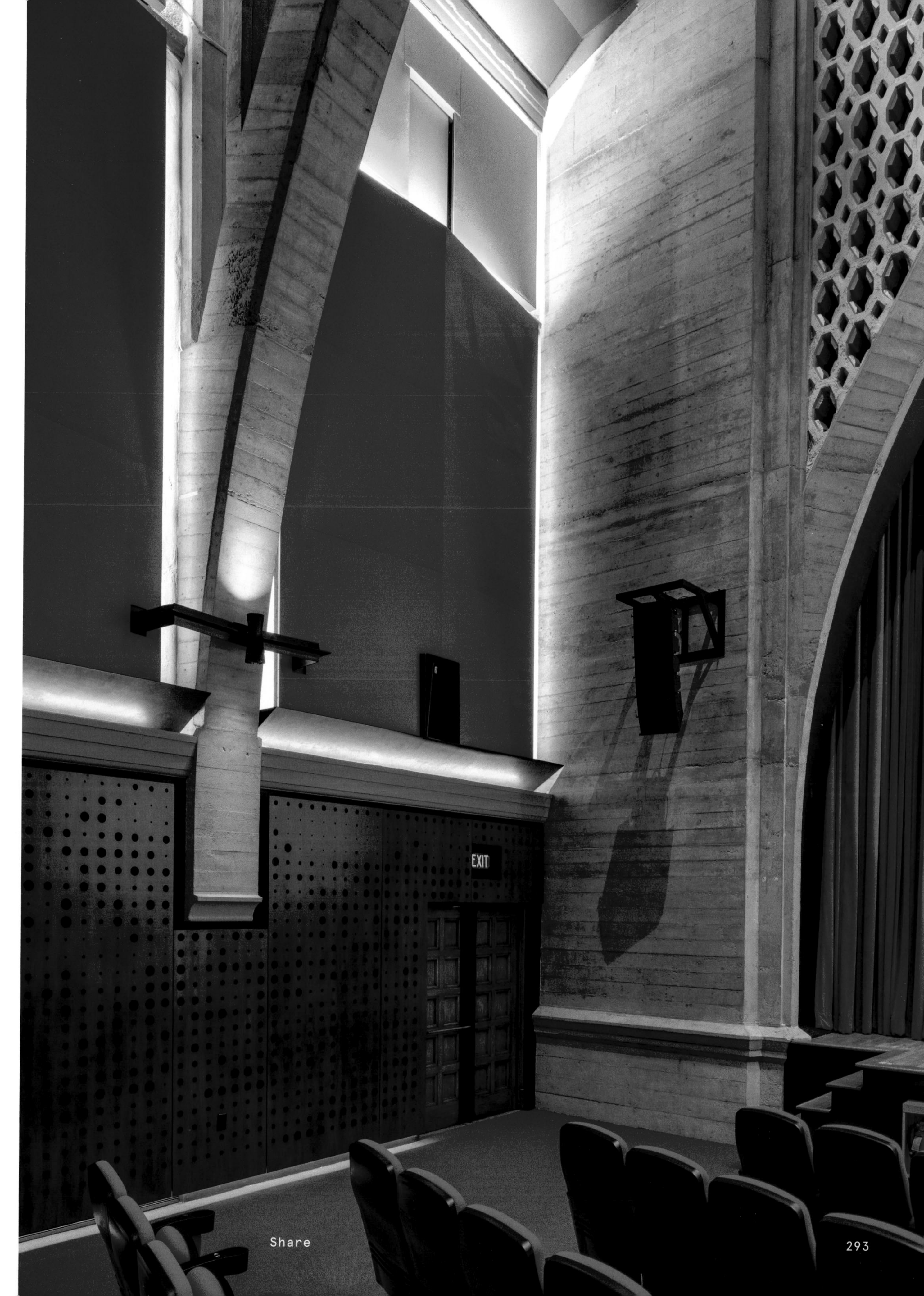
EXIT

Clubhouse assembly space before transformation

EXIT

EXIT
EXIT

Refurbished projection room

Cabaret Room on basement level

Original men's restroom from 1929

COURT F HONOR
WILSON C. P. JONES
CHARLES J. OREILLY
JAMES F BRADLEY

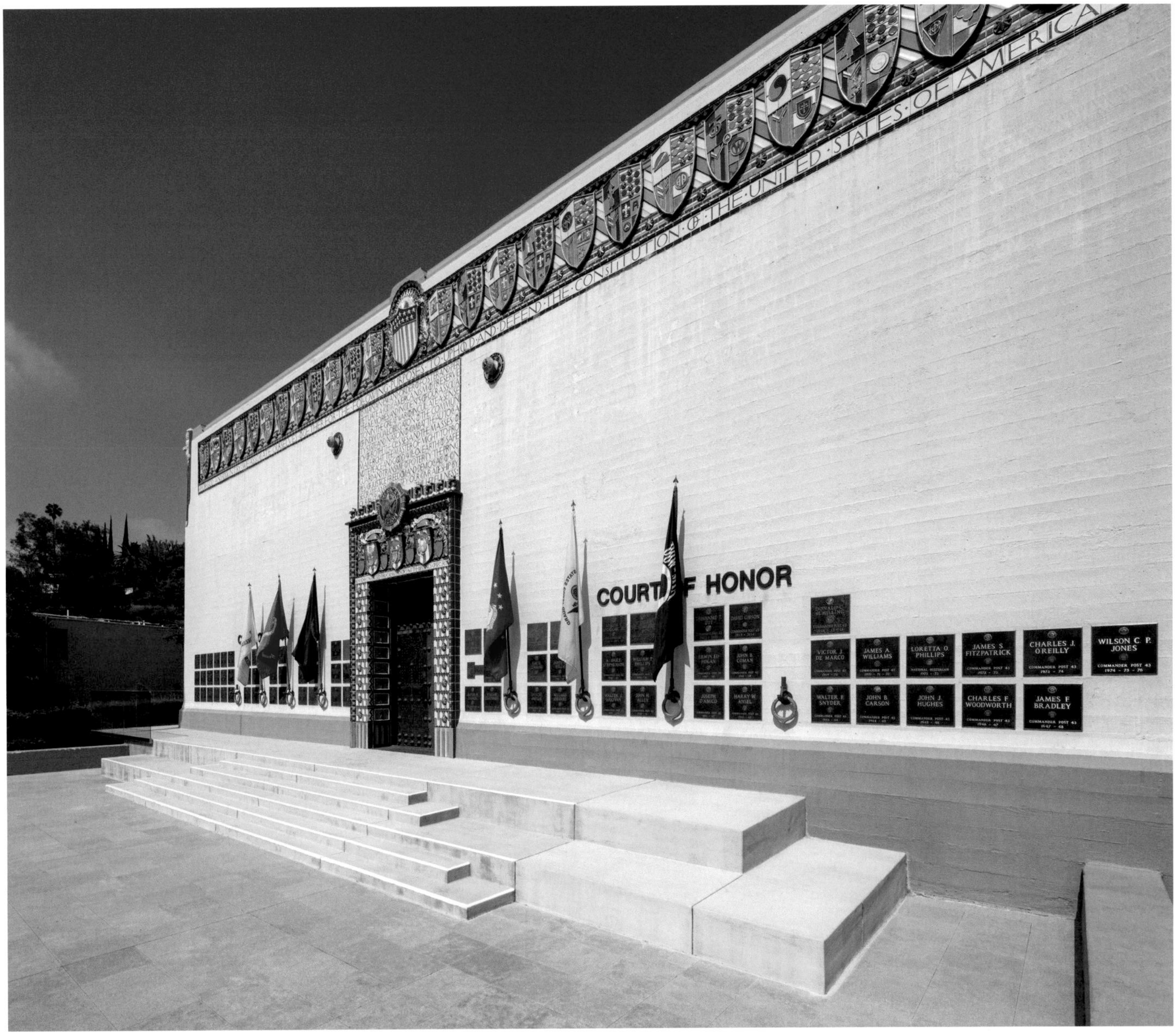

SITE PLAN

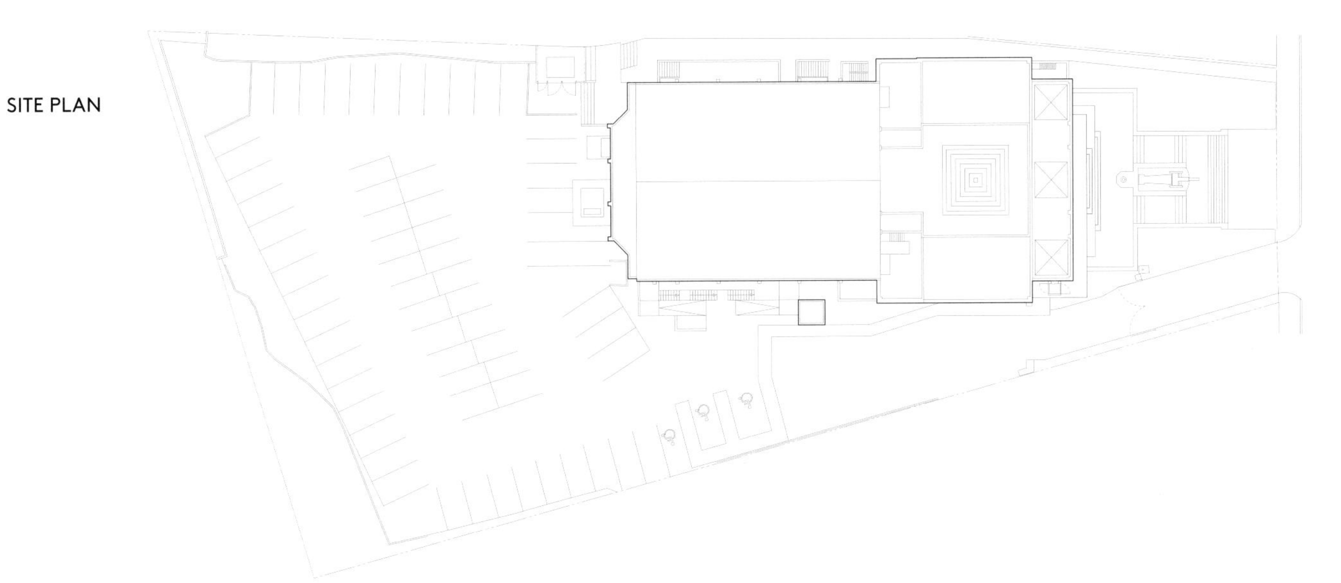

Front facade before renovation

Historic photograph from Highland Boulevard, early 20th century

Planned main entrance canopy

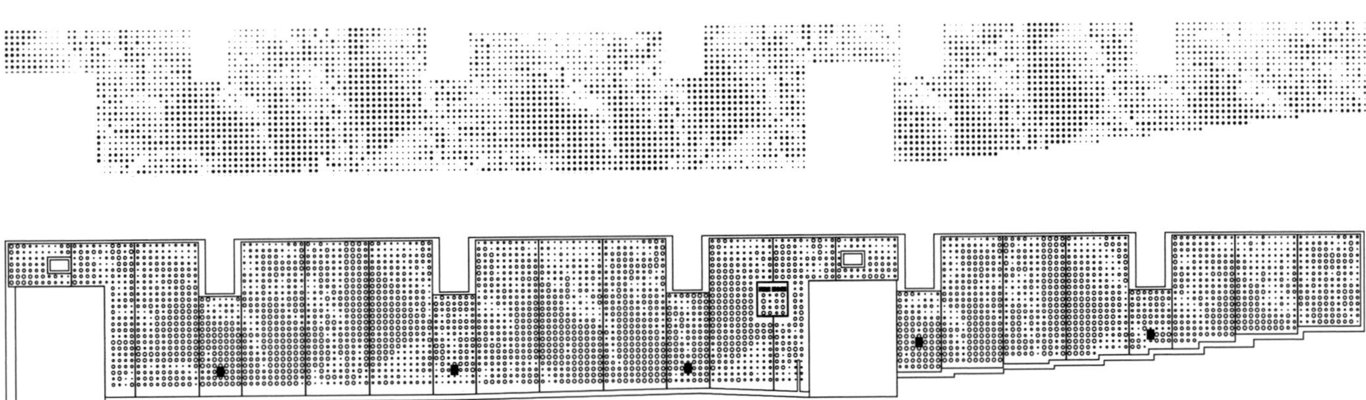

Perforated acoustic wood paneling

Marunouchi Piccadilly Multiplex
Tokyo, Japan

The Marunouchi Piccadilly Theaters, the flagship of the Shochiku Multiplex chain, are situated in a prominently located commercial highrise building in Ginza, Tokyo. The large theaters have a long and rich history and a loyal following, but the complex was in need of a contemporary update.

Besides dividing up the balcony of the larger theater into two additional smaller private screening rooms and updating the presentation technology, the focus of the remodel was on the lobbies and on the approach and perception by the public. That latter part was the scope of our design.

Inspiration for these public spaces came from vintage movie palaces in Hollywood and downtown Los Angeles. Built during the silent film era, they combine a rich and layered design with a classic and solid appearance. The goal was to emulate the richness and excitement of these places in contemporary fashion.

The theaters are located deep inside the building, and the new design makes a virtue of that. The enclosed nature of the spaces contributes to the desired calming effect, remote from the bustling world outside, and prepares the visitor for a unique experience. The way the theater spaces are carved out from the mass of the building reminds one of the spaces inside the great pyramids of Egypt, or in an even more primal way, of caves inside a mountain. The design metaphorically alludes to these natural phenomena. The lobbies will be modeled after the cavities and passageways of underground caverns, with elements recalling features found there.

The floor openings between the levels will be enlarged, offering glimpses from floor to floor. The layers of enrichment and the spatial articulations will be made by the modulated walls and ceilings, the signage, and video monitors. Lighting will be reminiscent of stalactites, bridging the levels through the openings with suspended fixtures and with indirect lights, hinting at cracks to the outside.

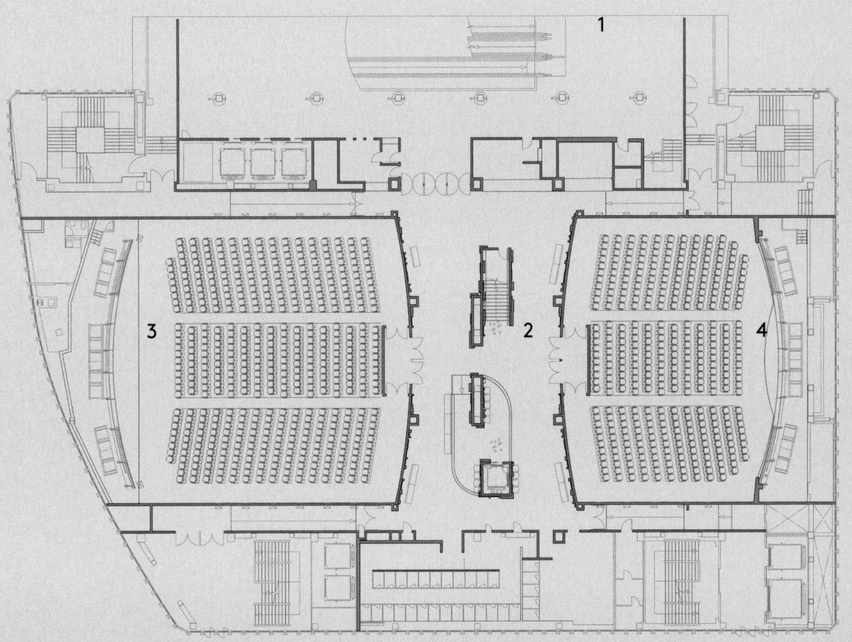

FLOOR PLAN THEATERS

1 Building Lobby
2 Theater Lobby Lower Level
3 Piccadilly Theater 1
4 Piccadilly Theater 2

日本の
いちばん
長い日

1

Existing project site

6 Appendix

Biographies

Bruce Botnick is a music producer and recording engineer. Credits in popular music include Beach Boys *Pet Sounds* – Good Vibrations, *The Doors*, Love – *Forever Changes*, MC5, Captain Beefheart, Dave Mason, The Rolling Stones, Neil Young, The Supremes, Marvin Gaye, Stevie Wonder, Weather Report, Earth Wind & Fire, Eddie Money, Kenny Loggins, Steve Perry, Sergio Mendez & Brazil '66, Tim Buckley, Crazy Horse, Buffalo Springfield. Over a period of 25 years, he recorded and produced well over 100 motion picture music scores with composer Jerry Goldsmith. In addition, he recorded and produced motion picture music scores for David Newman, John Williams, Alan Menken, James Newton Howard, Hans Zimmer, and Quincy Jones. Some of his music for film credits include: *Star Trek The Motion Picture, Total Recall, Basic Instinct, Rudy, Aladdin, Beauty and The Beast, The Lion King, E.T., The Color Purple, Caddy Shack, Poltergeist, Indiana Jones and The Temple of Doom, Gremlins, Rambo and The Sum of All Fears.* He was part of the original team for the original soundtrack album of *Mary Poppins.* Bruce produced and recorded the Broadway original cast recordings of *Beauty and the Beast, The Little Mermaid, Christmas Carol, National Lampoon's Lemmings and* Grammy Award winning *Lenny.*

David Goggin (aka Mr. Bonzai) is an award-winning photographer, music journalist, and author. He has written over 1,000 articles for magazines in the US, Europe, and Asia and has published numerous books, including *Studio Life* (Mix, 1984), *Hal Blaine and The Wrecking Crew* (Mix, 1992) *The Sound of Money* (Focal, 2000) *Faces of Music* (Cengage, 2006) *Music Smarts* (Berklee Press, 2009) and *John Lennon's Tooth* (BookBaby, 2012). His articles and photos have appeared in *Rolling Stone, The New York Times, Los Angeles Times, Billboard, Mix, EQ, Keyboard, Daily Variety, Hollywood Reporter, Los Angeles Magazine, Disney Channel Magazine, Sound & Recording,* and *Relix,* among others.

Peter Grueneisen is the founder and principal of nonzero\architecture and studio bau:ton, its media production facilities division. Trained in Switzerland and in the US, he holds an M. Arch. from the Southern California Institute of Architecture (SCI-Arc) and is a Fellow of the American Institute of Architects. He owns Greeniron Constructs, an architect-led design-build firm, building many of nonzero's projects. His clients range from families, individuals, and private companies to major film and music studios and national and international organizations. Peter is a multiple AIA and TEC award winner. He has lectured and taught in the US and abroad and is the author of *Soundspace: Architecture for Sound and Vision.* He has recently joined the board of the acclaimed classical music series *Jacaranda Music.* He is married and has two grown-up daughters.

Craig Hodgetts is known for employing an imaginative weave of high technology and storytelling to invigorate his designs, producing an architecture that embraces contemporary ideology, information culture, and evolving lifestyles. With a broad-ranging background in theater arts, automotive engineering, and architecture, he brings a singular synergy to the design of challenging environments. Craig has created legacy projects for the California Institute of the Arts, ArtCenter College, and Occidental College. His creative direction on a celebrated exhibition showcasing the Case Study program was followed by a series of landmark civic and cultural facilities including the Hollywood Bowl and the UCLA Gateway. Craig is a professor at the UCLA Graduate School of Architecture and Urban Planning, and was a Founding Dean of the School of Design at the California Institute of the Arts. A prolific writer, he has contributed essays and observations to the *Los Angeles Times and Cosmopolitan Magazine,* as well as signature books on science fiction icon Syd Mead and architect James Stirling. He has been granted patents for a mobile logistics center, a prefabricated classroom, and an evacuated tube structure for the hyperloop system.

Paul Lieberstein is a writer, director, and actor working in television and film. Best known for his work on *The Office: An American Workplace,* where he played Toby Flenderson as well as writing, producing, and directing. He also wrote, directed, and acted in the feature film *Song Of Back And Neck* and the soon to be released Audible original series *The Captain.*

Janine Poreba is an ESL instructor at Santa Monica College. Born and raised on Manhattan's Lower East Side, she moved to Los Angeles twelve years ago after attending graduate school in Monterey, CA.

Sam Lubell is a writer based in New York. He has written ten books about architecture for *Phaidon, Rizzoli, Metropolis Books, Monacelli Press* and *ORO Editions.* He writes for *The New York Times, The Los Angeles Times, Architectural Digest, Wallpaper, Dwell, Wired, The Atlantic, Metropolis, Architectural Record, The Architect's Newspaper, Architect Magazine,* and other publications. He co-curated the exhibition *Never Built New York* at the Queens Museum and *Never Built Los Angeles* at the A+D Architecture and Design Museum.

Brian Riordan is a two-time Grammy and four-time Emmy Award winning re-recording mixer, music mixer, musician, and entrepreneur. He is the founder and CEO of Levels Audio, a leading postproduction sound facility located in the heart of Hollywood, California. Started in 1999, Levels provides full sound packages for music, television, and film. Riordan is married and is the proud father of three daughters. While continuing to focus on growing his business, Riordan founded the Hollywood Compassion Coalition, a 501(c)(3) nonprofit organization. This came into focus through the combination of his daily meditation practice, inspiring conversations with like-minded people, and ultimately, a life-changing trip to India where he spent a week in the company of His Holiness, the 14th Dalai Lama. There, he saw his purpose with complete clarity – to take his twenty-five years of industry experience and personal network of Hollywood professionals and combine them with social scientists and contemplative masters to create a powerful synergy in an effort to make a positive and lasting impact on the world.

Thomas Aujero Small is the President and CEO of the public/private partnership Culver City Forward. He was formerly the mayor of Culver City and currently serves on the City Council. He also serves on the board of the renowned Southern California concert series *Jacaranda Music.* His home, Residence for a Briard, was designed by the architect Whitney Sander to be environmentally sustainable and to host chamber music concerts. He lives with his wife Joanna Brody, their two children, and two giant sheep dogs.

Michael Webb has authored more than twenty books on architecture and design, most recently *Architects' Houses* and a memoir *Moving Around: A Lifetime of Wandering,* while contributing essays to many more. He is also a regular contributor to leading journals in the US and Europe. Growing up in London, he was an editor at *The Times* and *Country Life* before moving to the US where he directed film programs for the American Film Institute and curated a Smithsonian exhibition on Hollywood.

Hans Zimmer has scored more than 200 projects across all mediums which, combined, have grossed more than 28 billion dollars at the worldwide box office. Zimmer has been honored with an Academy Award, two Golden Globes, three Grammys, an American Music Award, and a Tony Award. Zimmer's work highlights over the past few years include *Widows,* which reteamed the composer with director Steve McQueen after previously working together on the critically acclaimed *12 Years A Slave; Blade Runner 2049* which he co-scored alongside Benjamin Wallfisch and earned Grammy, BAFTA, and Critics' Choice nominations for Best Score; and Christopher Nolan's *Dunkirk* which earned him nominations for an Academy Award, Grammy Award, Golden Globe, BAFTA Award, and Critics' Choice Award. Other notable scores include *Gladiator, The Thin Red Line, As Good as It Gets, Rain Man, The Dark Knight trilogy, Inception, Thelma and Louise, Black Hawk Down* and *The Last Samurai.* Zimmer most recently scored the live action remake of *The Lion King,* for which he received a Grammy nomination for Best Score Soundtrack for Visual Media. The film, which was released by Disney on July 19, 2019, grossed over $1.7 billion at the box office. Upcoming projects include *Wonder Woman 1984* set to be released by Warner Bros. June 5, 2020, *Top Gun: Maverick,* which will be released by Paramount on June 26, 2020, and the latest James Bond film *No Time to Die,* which will be released by MGM on April 10, 2020. Recently, Zimmer completed highly successful Hans Zimmer Live tour stops across Asia and Australia and continues to perform concerts around the globe, including an upcoming European tour beginning in February 2021.

Selected Works

Burt Lancaster Theatre 2019
Commercial Mix Stage
Remodel
Sony Pictures Entertainment
Culver City, CA

MTSU 2019
Music Education Studios
Middle Tennessee State University
Murfreesboro, TN

Federal 2019
Residential Studios and Residence
Atli and Anna Örvarsson
Los Angeles, CA

Latigo 2019
New Residence
Dino and Candice Meneghin
Malibu, CA

Mix 1–29 2019
Commercial Mix Stage
20th Century Fox
Century City, CA

Stage 6 2019
Commercial Mix Stage
NBC Universal
Universal City, CA

Oxy 2019
Music / Media Education Studios
Occidental College
Eagle Rock, CA

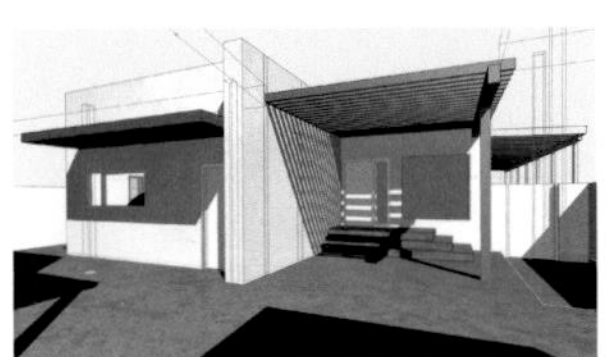

Fair Park 2019
Residential Studio
Adam Schoenberg
Eagle Rock, CA

Deca 2019
Commercial Recording Studio
A.R. Rahman
Chennai, India

Ruberta 2019
Residential Studio
Michael Kramer
Glendale, CA

Scoring Lab 2018–2020
Composing and Mix Facility
Benjamin Wallfisch
Santa Monica, CA

Glenview 2018
Residential Studio
Philip and Maia White
Glendale, CA

Fire Stations 1 and 3 2018–2020
Partial Fire Station Remodels
City of Beverly Hills
Beverly Hills, CA

Marunouchi Piccadilly 2018 – 2020
Cinema Remodel
Shochiku Multiplex Theatres
Tokyo, Japan
→ page 307

Dixon Hall 2018
Music Education Studio (un-built)
Tulane University
New Orleans, LA

AFM Local 47 2018
Rehearsal Building (un-built)
American Federation of Musicians
Burbank, CA

Apo Leo 2012–2019
Music Education Studio
University of Hawaii, Maui College
Kahului, HI

Mar Vista 2017–2020
New Residence
Giancarlo Skolnick
Mar Vista, CA
→ page 75

Chicago Scoring 2017 –2018
Design Concept (un-built)
Third Coast Music
Chicago, IL
→ page 227

Fox Audio 99 2017
Post Production Facility (un-built)
20th Century Fox Audio Services
Los Angeles, CA

Psomas 2017–2020
Residential Studio Addition
Nathan and Lara Whitehead
Mar Vista, CA

Barry 2017 –2020
Residential Addition
James and Kathy Peterson
Mar Vista, CA

Last House on Mulholland 2017
Competition Entry
Hollywood, CA

Momentum 2011–2014; 2017–2020
Composing and Recording Studios
Momentum RLP, William Ross
Santa Monica; Woodland Hills, CA
→ page 171

OpenAir Stages 2016–2018
Outdoor Film Shooting Stage
(un-built)
MegaMace
Los Angeles, CA

Elbo 2013–2015; 2016–2019
Composing and Recording Studios
Theodore Shapiro
Ludwig Goransson
Glendale, CA
→ page 161

American Legion 2016–2019
Clubhouse and Movie Theater
American Legion Hollywood Post 43
Hollywood, CA
→ page 291

Electric 2008; 2016–2017
Film Screening / Mix Room
Film Production Facility
Electric Entertainment
Hollywood, CA

Mulholland 2016–2017
Residential Screening Room
Dean Devlin
Los Angeles, CA

Palmer 2016–2018
Residential Studio
Matt Kajcienski
Glassell Park, CA

Molino 2016
Residential Studio
Ted Reedy
Los Angeles, CA

West Valley 2016–2018
Residential Studio Building
Mick Schultz
Tarzana, CA
→ page 85

Levels Audio 2005–2010; 2015–2018
Commercial Postproduction Facility
Brian Riordan
Hollywood, CA
→ page 243

Green Roof Park 2015–2017
Public Park
City of Santa Monica Airport
Santa Monica, CA

PCH 2015
Residential Screening Room Consultation
David Geffen
Malibu, CA

Tigertail 2015
Residential Studio
Henry Jackman
Los Angeles, CA

Noise Nest 2015–2019
Commercial Recording Studio
Strz Enterprises
Los Angeles, CA

Barking Owl 2015–2016
Commercial Postproduction Studio
Barking Owl
Los Angeles, CA

Manhattan Beach Pier 2015–2018
Pier Roundhouse Remodel
City of Manhattan Beach
Manhattan Beach, CA

NPR West 2002; 2015–2018
Broadcasting and Production Facility
National Public Radio
Culver City, CA
Soundspace 04:190

The Barn 2015–2018
Residential Studio
Michael Marquart
Malibu, CA
→ page 99

Activision Audio 2014
Postproduction Studios (un-built)
Activision Blizzard
Playa del Rey, CA

Consulate Villa 2014
Residential Remodel
EDA Switzerland
Hancock Park, CA

Wazemoos 2014–2016
Farmhouse Residence Remodel
Kurt and Therese Grueneisen
Diemtigen, Switzerland

Newbury Park 2014–2016
Residential Studio Consultation
John Fogerty
Thousand Oaks, CA

Sphere 2014–2016
Commercial Recording Studio (un-built)
Francesco Cameli
Burbank, CA

Monmouth 2014–2016; 2018–2020
Residential Remodel and Addition
Garage and Guesthouse
Ed and Aline Holzwarth
Durham, NC

Barrington 2013–2014
Residential Studio
James Levine
Los Angeles, CA

Shochiku 2013–2015
Commercial Postproduction Studios
Shochiku Corporation
Tokyo, Japan
→ page 263

Insomniac 2013–2015
Residential Studio (un-built)
Pasquale Rotella
Las Vegas, NV

Sierra Mar 2013–2016
Hillside Residence (un-built)
Mindy Kaling
Los Angeles, CA

NBC Access Hollywood 2013–2014
TV Production Facility Relocation
(un-built)
NBC Universal
Studio City, CA

Windmark 2012–2015
Commercial Studio Facility
Expansion
Michael Marquart
Santa Monica, CA
→ page 199

Main Street 2012
Personal Composing Studio
Toby Chu
Venice, CA

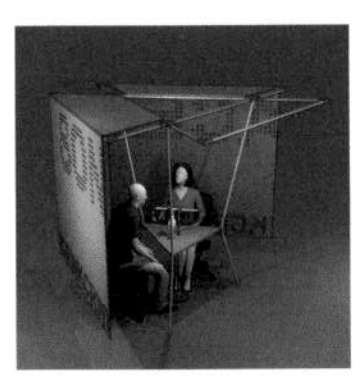

Sonic Trace 2012
Mobile Recording Booth
Competition Entry, KCRW
Santa Monica, CA

9th Street / 14th Street 2008; 2012
Residential Recording Studio
Studio Facility Remodel
Steve Jablonsky
Santa Monica, CA

Extasy 2012–2017
Commercial Studio Facility
Remodel
YSK Enterprises, Yoshiki Hayashi
Hollywood, CA

WoodAward 2011
Furniture Design Competition
Switzerland

Hatteras 2011
Residential Studio
Geoff Zanelli
Woodland Hills, CA

NBCU 2160-07 2011–2016
Commercial Postproduction
Studios
NBC Universal
Studio City, CA

Unterschall 2011–2013
Residential Studio and Landscape
Charlie Clouser
Malibu, CA

RCP 1523 / 1551 2011–2014
Commercial Studio Building
Remote Control Productions
Santa Monica, CA
→ page 141

The Farm LA 2011–2012
Commercial Postproduction Studio
The Farm Group, London
Hollywood, CA
→ page 255

Zumirez 2011–2015
Residential Studio Building
Malibu, CA

Montana Film 2010–2011
Film Production Studio Complex
(un-built)
Seth Allman Bloom
Missoula, MT

DreamWorks 2008–2012
Recording and Postproduction
Facility
DreamWorks Animation SKG
Glendale, CA
→ page 207

Wardley Cottage 2010
Residential Studio
Rupert Gregson-Williams
England, UK

Skyline 2010–2012
Residential Hardscape and
Landscape
Brian Riordan
Hollywood, CA

Edinburgh 2009
Personal Composing Studio
A.R. Rahman
Los Angeles, CA

Red Door 2003; 2009
Residential Studios
John Merchant
Miami, FL; Murfreesboro, TN

Stanford 2009
Personal Composing Studio
James Peterson
Santa Monica, CA

Crestwood Hills 2009–2012
New Residence
Paul Lieberstein and Janine Poreba
Los Angeles, CA
→ page 55

Innovative Transit 2009
Competition Entry
Los Angeles, CA

740 Sound 2009–2012
Sound Design and Recording
Studio
Scott Ganary
Playa Vista, CA
→ page 271

Silver Lake 2008
Residential Recording Studio
Joseph Gordon-Levitt
Los Angeles, CA

CityTV 2008
Municipal Cable TV Station
City of Santa Monica
Santa Monica, CA

Dakota Pictures 2007–2008
Production Office Facade
North Hollywood, CA

Red Amp 2007–2008
Commercial Recording Studio
9WG Studios
Richmond, VA
→ page 215

Saint Charles 2007–2008
Residential Composing Studio
Terence Blanchard
New Orleans, LA

Sonic Mayhem 2007–2008
Residential Recording Studio
Sascha Dikiciyan
Los Angeles, CA

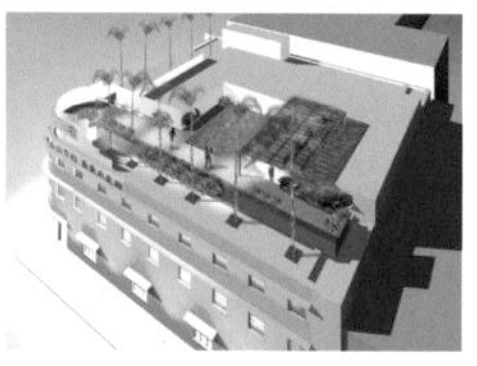

Record Plant SOBE 2001–2003; 2007
Commercial and Recording Studio
Complex (un-built)
Rick Stevens
Miami Beach, FL

Clearstory 2007–2008
Residential Recording Studio
John Rodd
Culver City, CA

Octavia 2007–2016
Residential Recording Studio
Michael Wandmacher
Encino, CA

Music Shed 2007
Film Scoring Stage (un-built)
New Orleans, LA

Laurel Ridge 2007–2008
Residential Art Studio Building
(un-built)
LeRoi Moore
Charlottesville, VA

Art Institute 2007–2008
Media Production Teaching Studio
Art Institute Music and Audio
Recording Program
Santa Monica, CA

Moldex 2006–2007
Multimedia Conference Room
Culver City, CA

**RCP 1531/
1542/1547** 2005–2007; 2006–2009
Composing and Postproduction
Studios
Film Scoring Stage (un-built)
Remote Control Productions
Santa Monica, CA
→ page 119

RCP 1537 2006–2009
Commercial Studio Building
Remote Control Productions
Santa Monica, CA
→ page 131

Fox DVD 2006–2007
Postproduction Studio
20th Century Fox
Century City, CA

GSN 2006–2007
Television Production Studio
Game Show Network
Culver City, CA

EA 2006
Postproduction Studios (un-built)
Electronic Arts Video Games
Redwood Shores, CA

Molino Lofts 2006
Residential Studio (un-built)
Michael Mangiamele
Los Angeles, CA

**Newman
Scoring** 1995–1997; 2006–2008
Film Scoring Facility
20th Century Fox
Century City, CA

NC Soft 2006–2009
Postproduction Studios
NC Soft Video Games
Aliso Viejo, CA

Linwood 2005; 2006–2007
Residential Studio Addition
(un-built) Remodel of Gordon
Kaufman designed Residence
LeRoi Moore
Los Feliz, CA

Broadcast 2005
Live Feed Studio
Pepperdine University
Malibu, CA

AIX 2005–2006
Audio Mixing and Mastering Studio
Mark Waldrep
Los Angeles, CA

JNH Studios 1996–1999; 2005–2006
Composing and Recording Studio
Facility
James Newton Howard
Santa Monica, CA
→ page 179

Horizon 2005
Residential Studio
Mark Morgan
Malibu, CA

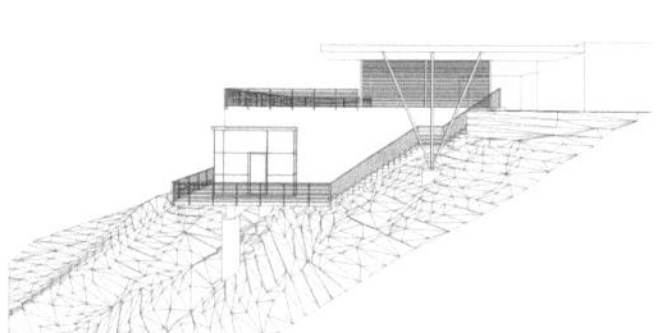

Roscomare 2005
Residential Studio Building
(un-built)
Chris Walden
Bel Air, CA

e-teepee 2004
Competition Entry 'Home on the
Range'
American Institute of Architects

Blend + Bottle 2004
Wine Tasting Retail Concept
(un-built)
Napa Valley, CA

Sigma Sound 2004
Commercial Recording Studios
(un-built)
Philadelphia, PA

Trino 2004
Bathroom Remodel to Richard
Neutra designed Residence
Pacific Palisades, CA

CMX 2003–2004
Commercial Postproduction Studios
Century Productions
Las Vegas, NV

Space X 2003–2004
Executive Office Addition (un-built)
Space-X, Elon Musk
El Segundo, CA

Hoofddorp 2003–2005
Executive Film Screening Room
The Walt Disney Company
Amsterdam, Netherlands

Kriens Shopping Center 2003
Invited Competition Entry, Retail Concept for New Mall
Kriens, Switzerland

The Idea Place 2003–2004
Commercial Postproduction Studio Facility
Warner Bros Studios
Burbank, CA

Middle Ear 2003
Commercial Studio Remodel (un-built)
The Bee Gees
South Beach, FL

Miami Beach 2003
Residential Studio Building (un-built)
Barry Gibb
Miami Beach, FL

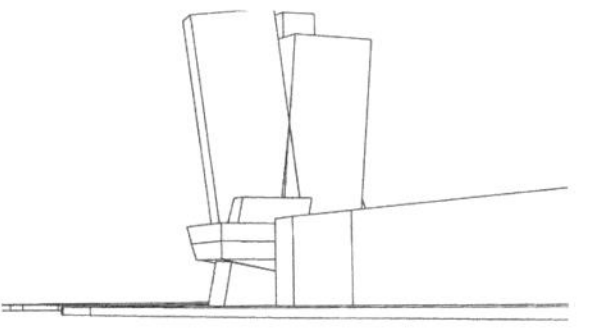

Dublin Docklands 2003
Competition Entry, Commercial and Residential Tower
U2
Dublin, Ireland

Stade de Suisse 2003
Invited Competition Entry, Plaza and Retail Concept
Bern, Switzerland

Lime 2002–2004
Commercial Postproduction Studio Facility
Santa Monica, CA

Albemarle County 2002–2003
Residential Studio
Carter Beauford
Charlottesville, VA

UnitEye 2002–2003
Personal Recording Studio
Bruce Botnick
Ojai, CA

CRA 2002–2003
Music and Audio Production School (un-built)
Center for the Recording Arts
North Hollywood, CA
Soundspace 04:204

Villa Costera 2003–2012
Residential Addition and Remodel
Michael and Donna Sedgwick
Malibu, CA

Arlington Heights 2003
Residential Studio
Ian Dye
Los Angeles, CA

Disney Paris 2002
Executive Film Screening Room
The Walt Disney Company
Marne-la-Vallée, France

DMB 2002
Rehearsal and Recording Studio
Dave Matthews Band
Charlottesville, VA
Soundspace 04:210

Shi-Ga Museum of Art 2001
Open International Competition Entry
Tomihiro, Japan
Soundspace 01:013

Boom Boom Room 2001–2004
Commercial Recording Studio
Will Smith
Burbank, CA,

Full Sail 2001–2003
Film Dubbing Theater and Campus Master Plan
Full Sail University
Winter Park, FL
Soundspace 04:196, 04:198

Studio Atlantis 1998–2002
Commercial Recording Studios
Jon Newkirk
Hollywood, CA
Soundspace 04:139

Queens Museum of Art 2001
Open International Competition Entry, First Alternate
Queens, NY
Soundspace 04:082

Canyon 2001–2002
Elementary School Auditorium Remodel
Canyon Charter School
Los Angeles, CA

MAP 2001
Residential Recording Studio (un-built)
Marc Anthony
Brookville, NY

First Street 2003–2004
Residential Addition and Remodel
Kimi Sato
Redondo Beach, CA

Face the Music 2001–2003
Commercial Recording Studio
New York, NY

LMP 2001–2003
Residential Recording Studio
James Linahon
Claremont, CA

Blue Jay 2001
Residential Studio Remodel
Robin Thicke
Hollywood, CA

Zona Playa 2000–2001
Commercial Postproduction Studio (un-built)
LA Studios
Santa Monica, CA

Studio 800 2000–2001
Residential Studio
Tom Hormel
Pacific Palisades, CA
Soundspace 04:210

Tareco 2000–2001
Residence Remodel and Addition
Jon Newkirk Family
Hollywood, CA

Euro Disney 2000
Audio Production Studio for Theme Park
Marne-la-Vallée, France

Cheyenne 2000
Videoconference and Presentation Room
Cheyenne Productions
Santa Monica, CA

BridgeCo 2000
Tech Startup Engineering Lab
Zürich, Switzerland

Thinktank 2000
New Media Advertising Agency (un-built)
Chicago, IL
Soundspace 04:220

First Look Art 2000
Art Retail and Internet Sales Concept (un-built)
Los Angeles, CA

Kokoro 2000–2002
Residential Studio
Ben Schultz
Valley Village, CA
Soundspace 04:208

Supertracks 2000
New Media Production Facility (un-built)
Santa Monica, CA
Soundspace 04:218

Launch 1999; 2000
Postproduction Studios
Launch Media
Santa Monica, CA; New York, NY

Zuma 2000
Residential Studio Consultation
David Newman
Malibu, CA

MI / Campus Hollywood / UTB TV 1996–2000
Recording School Teaching Studio
Television Station and Campus Master Plan
Master Plan and Acting Studio (un-built)
Musicians Institute
Hollywood, CA
Soundspace 04:202

Palos Verdes Art Center 2000
Open International Competition Entry
Palos Verdes, CA
Soundspace 01:012

Via de la Paz 1995–1998; 1999–2002
Remodel and Addition to Richard Neutra designed Residence
Bruce and Marie Botnick
Jeff Ayeroff and Marty Longbine
Pacific Palisades, CA
→ page 33

4MC 1999
Music Recording Studio
Singapore, Singapore

Helsinki Music Center 1999
Open International Competition Entry
Helsinki, Finland
Soundspace 04:074

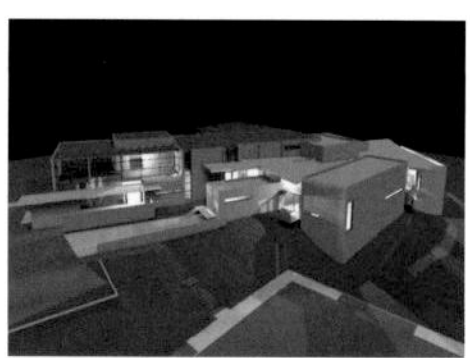

Studio 1314 1999–2000
Commercial Recording Studio Complex (un-built)
Melisma
Atlanta, GA
Soundspace 04:148

Pennsylvania 1997–2000
Composing and Recording Studio
Christophe Beck
Santa Monica, CA
Soundspace 04:187

Bellagio 1999
Personal Screening Room
Michael Bay
Bel Air, CA

Graz 1999
Broadcast Studios
Wirtschaftskammer Steiermark
Graz, Austria

Buena Park 1999
Residential Studio
Gregg Field and Monica Mancini
Studio City, CA
Soundspace 04:208

Musikvergnuegen 1999
Music Production Studio Remodel
Walter Werzowa
Hollywood, CA

Promise 1999
Commercial Recording Studio Facility
Taipei, Taiwan

Wilshire Stages 1998–1999
Film Mix Stages Remodel
Los Angeles, CA

Sarde 1999
Film Mix Stage
Philippe Sarde
Paris, France

Live Oak 1999
Personal Screening Room
David Vogel
Los Feliz, CA

Olive 1999
Composing and Recording Studio Facility
John Debney
Burbank, CA

East Side Film 1998
Commercial Postproduction Studios
New York, NY

Audiophase 1998–1999
Film Postproduction Studio Facility
Paris, France

Bell Canyon 1998–2000
New Residence (un-built)
Howard Levine Family
Bell Canyon, CA

Chalice 1998–1999
Commercial Recording Studios
Ben Tao
Hollywood, CA

Howard Schwartz 1994; 1998
Commercial Postproduction Studios
New York, NY

USA Network 1998
Television Broadcast Facility (un-built)
Hollywood, CA

Master P 1998–1999
Residential Recording Studio
Percy Miller
Baton Rouge, LA

Sony Music Japan 1998–2001
Commercial Recording Studios
Sony Music Entertainment Japan
Tokyo, Japan
Soundspace 04:130

Margarita Mix 1998–1999
Commercial Postproduction Studio
Facility
LA Studios
Santa Monica, CA

DARP 1991; 1998–1999
Commercial Recording Studios
Dallas Austin
Atlanta, GA

Luminous Sound 1998–1999
Commercial Recording Studios
Dallas, TX
Soundspace 04:152

Rotor / Metropol 1998
New Media Production Studios
(un-built)
Los Angeles, CA

No Limit 1998–1999
Commercial Recording Studio
Complex (un-built)
Master P
Baton Rouge, LA
Soundspace 04:162

O'Henry 1998–1999
Commercial Recording Studio
Remodel
Hank Sanicola
Burbank, CA,

Green Dragon 1997–1998
Creative Offices, Adaptive Re-use
(un-built)
Amsterdam, Netherlands

The Complex 1993; 1997
Commercial Recording Studios
Los Angeles, CA

Rockland 1997–1998
Commercial Recording Studio
Complex (un-built)
Chicago, IL
See Soundspace 04:119

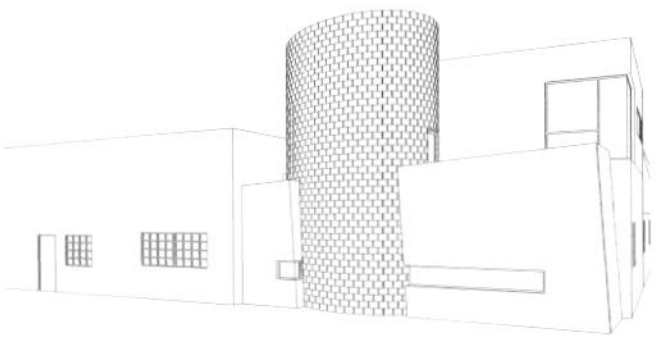

Audiobanks 1997–1998
Commercial Postproduction Studio
Facility
Ear to Ear
Santa Monica, CA

EMP 1997–1998
Entertainment Ride Concept for
Frank Gehry designed building
Digital Domain
Seattle, WA

Duran Studios 1997–1998
Film Postproduction Studios
Paris, France

City Switch 1997–2000
Linked Entertainment Venues
(un-built)
Amsterdam, London, Berlin
Soundspace 04:216

Wonderland 1997–1998
Recording Studio Expansion
(un-built)
Stevie Wonder
Los Angeles, CA

Lombard 1997
Residential Recording Studio
John Frizzell
Pacific Palisades, CA

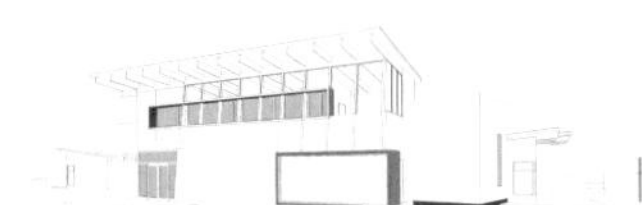

Our House 1997–1998
Commercial Recording Studio
Complex (un-built)
Barry Rose
Lemont, IL
Soundspace 04:129

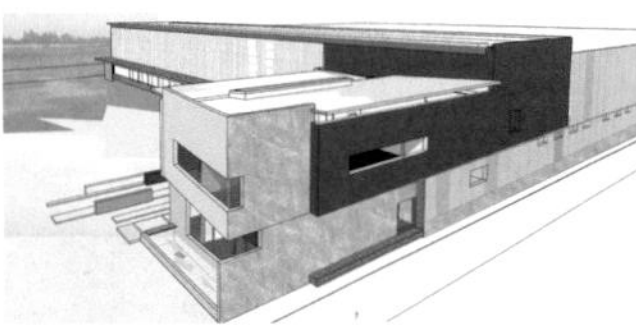

Antara 1997
Commercial Refrigeration and
Distribution Center (un-built)
Ho Chi Minh City, Vietnam

In Your Ear 1995–1999
Commercial Recording Studio
Facility
Richmond, VA

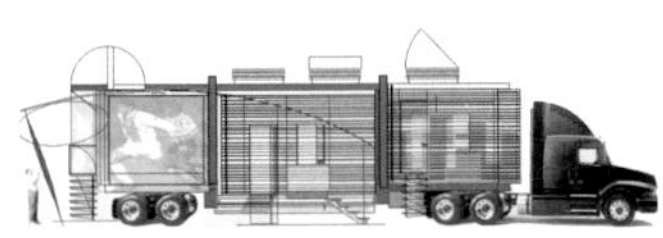

TF1 Truck 1997
Mobile Broadcasting Vehicle
Prototype
TF1 Television
Paris, France
Soundspace 04:192

TK Disk 1994–1999
Commercial Recording Studios
Tetsuya Komuro
Honolulu, HI
Soundspace 04:155

Mandeville 1996
Residential Studio
Patrick Williams
Brentwood, CA

Symphony 1996
Film Postproduction Studios
Buenos Aires, Argentina

X-Treme Mobile 1996
Mobile Audio Recording Truck
Seattle, WA

The Lair 1996
Residential Studio
Brian Austin Green
Hollywood, CA

Audio Resource 1996
New Residence and Studio
Tony Hugar
Honolulu, HI

Appleton 1996
Residential Studio Addition
(un-built)
Erin Davis
Venice, CA

Sound Matrix 1996
Commercial Rehearsal Studios
Fountain Valley, CA

Porno for Pyros 1996
Band Recording Studio
Perry Farrell
Venice, CA

Coral Springs 1996–1997
Residential Studio
James and Ron Last
Coral Springs, FL
Soundspace 04:208

Future Studios 1992; 1996–1997
Commercial Recording Studio
Teddy Riley
Virginia Beach, VA

Yello / Soundproof 1993; 1996–1997
Residential Studios
Dieter Meier
Malibu, CA; Los Feliz, CA
Soundspace 04:210

Fatima Records 1996
Commercial Recording Studio Facility
Bangkok, Thailand

Snoop 1996
Residential Studio
Calvin Broadus
Baton Rouge, LA

Rocktropolis / IHG 1995–1996
Internet Production and Broadcast Studios
Internet Holdings Group
Hollywood, CA

Counterpoint 1995–1996
Commercial Recording Studio Facility
Giancarlo Skolnick
Salt Lake City, UT
Soundspace 04:110

Brandon's Way 1997–1998
Commercial Recording Studios
Kenneth 'Babyface' Edmonds
Hollywood, CA
Soundspace 04:119

Mesmer Av 1995
Personal Recording Studio
David Blau
Culver City, CA

Tremens Film 1995–1996
Film Postproduction Facility
Vienna, Austria

Villa Muse 1995–2010
Film Production Studio Complex (un-built)
Jay Aaron Podolnick
Austin, TX

Anacapa 1995
Personal Recording and Production Studio
Prem Rawat
Malibu, CA

Embassy 1994
Commercial Recording Studio Facility
Peter Wolf
Weiler, Austria

EFX 1994
Commercial Postproduction Studio Facility
EFX Studios
Burbank, CA

Hyperbolic 1990 –1994; 2002
Personal Recording Studio
Walter Becker
Maui, HI

Chautauqua 1994–1995
Residential Studio
Murielle and Joel Hamilton, Musicians/Composers
Pacific Palisades, CA
Soundspace 04:210

LA Recording Workshop 1994
Music and Audio Production School
North Hollywood, CA

Sega 1994
Recording Studio Facility
Sega Video Games
San Francisco, CA

Leeway 1994
Personal Composing and Recording Studio
Santa Monica, CA

Syntrax Music 1994
Commercial Postproduction Studio
Pittsburgh, PA

Euphonix 1994
Recording and Production Test Facility
San Francisco, CA

Asymmetrical 1994–1997
Film Production Facility and Recording Studio
David Lynch
Hollywood, CA
Soundspace 04:178

ORF Vienna 1994–1996
Broadcast Control Rooms
ORF Austrian National Radio Network
Vienna, Austria

DubeyTunes 1994–1995; 1997
Commercial Postproduction Studios
San Francisco, CA

Estudios Churubusco 1994–1995
Commercial Film Dubbing and Mixing Stages Studio
Mexico City, Mexico

American Gramaphone 1994
Commercial Recording Studios
Omaha, NE

SSL 1995
Audio Equipment Presentation Studio
Solid State Logic
Hollywood, CA

VTU 1995
Commercial Recording Studio
Vietnam

Oceanway Nashville 1993 –1995
Commercial Recording Studio Facility
Nashville, TN

Costa del Sol 1993–1996
New Residence
David and Michelle Sack
Malibu, CA

Ground Control 1993
Commercial Recording Studio Remodel
Burbank, CA

Mega /Mega West 1993–1996
Music Recording Studio Facilities
Paris, France
Soundspace 04:116

Sunset Plaza 1993–1994
Residential Studio
Ice-T
Hollywood, CA
Soundspace 04:208

Royaltone 1992–1995
Commercial Recording Studio Facility
Alias Records
North Hollywood, CA
Soundspace 04:105

C+C Music 1992–1995
Commercial Recording Studios
C+C Music Factory
New York, NY

LaCoco 1992–1993
Commercial Recording Studios
L.A. Reid and Kenneth Edmonds
Atlanta, GA

X-Art 1992–1993
Music Recording Studio Facility
Pinkafeld, Austria
Soundspace 04:098

One on One 1992; 1995; 1997
Commercial Recording Studio Remodels
Yoshiki Hayashi
North Hollywood, CA

Swell 1992–1995
Audio and Video Postproduction Studio Facility
Swell Pictures / Swell Audio
Chicago, IL

The Record Plant 1991–1995
Commercial Recording Studios
Hollywood, CA
Soundspace 04:094

NRG 1991–1993
Commercial Recording Studio Remodel
North Hollywood, CA

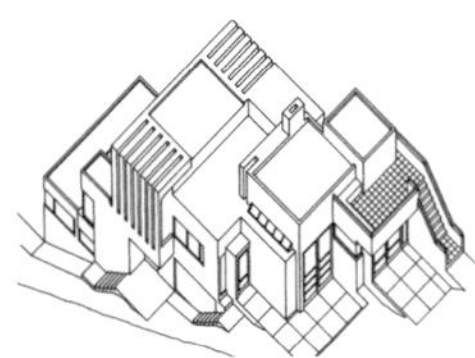

Elliot Residence 1991–1993
Addition to Rudolph Schindler designed Residence (un-built)
Dana Levy and Tish O'Connor
Los Angeles, CA

525 Post 1991–1995
Commercial Postproduction Studios
Hollywood, CA

Maui Island Recorders 1991–1992
Commercial Resort Recording Studio Complex (un-built)
Maui, HI

Goodnight LA 1991
Commercial Recording Studio
Keith Olsen
Calabasas, CA

Bad Animals 1991–1992
Commercial Recording Studio
Lawson Productions / Heart
Seattle, WA
Soundspace 04:090

Nuages 1991
Personal Recording Studio
Peter Frampton
North Hollywood, CA

Sierra Mar 1991–1992
Residential Rehearsal Studio
Stewart Copeland
Hollywood, CA

Quincy Jones Productions 1991
Acoustic Consultation
Burbank, CA

Pink Ton 1991
Commercial Recording Studio (un-built)
Juerg Naegeli
Solothurn, Switzerland

Park for the Swiss Abroad 1990
Competition Entry
Brunnen, Switzerland
Soundspace 01:013

Vestal 1990
Residential Studio Addition
Mike Diamond
Silver Lake, CA

Rosewood 1990–1993
Residential Second Floor Addition
Wayne and Noriko Peet
Mar Vista, CA

Toad Hall 1990
Personal Recording Studio
Bill Bottrell
Pasadena, CA

Klasky Csupo 1990–1991
Voice-over Recording Space
Klasky Csupo Animation Company
Hollywood, CA

Post Logic 1990–1995
Commercial Postproduction Studios
Hollywood, CA
Soundspace 04:169

Golden Lady 1990
Recording Studio Expansion (un-built)
Ron Isley and Angela Winbush
Hollywood, CA

Hancock 1990
Residential Studio
Bob Crewe
West Hollywood, CA

LaFace 1990–1991
Recording Studio Facility
L.A. Reid and Kenneth Edmonds
Atlanta, GA

Larmar 1989–1990
Residential Studio Addition
Craig Harris
Hollywood, CA

PHOTO CREDITS

American Legion Hollywood Post 43: p. 304 bottom right
Archiv Atelier 5, Bern: p. 16
Chloe Atkins: p. 324: Leeway
Bruce Botnick: p. 197
Andreas Bruckner: p. 193 bottom
Edward Colver: p. 124; p. 125; p. 184 top; p. 185; p. 190; p. 191; p. 192 bottom; p. 252; p. 253; p. 320: Newman Scoring; p. 321: Boom Boom; p. 322: MI; Buena Park; p. 323: Yello; p. 324: Sunset Plaza; p. 325: Royaltone; NRG
Stephan Doleschal: p. 325: X-Art
John Ellis: p. 37; p. 38; p. 45; p. 47; p. 48; p. 52; p. 53
David Franzen: p. 323: TK Disk
Denis Freppel: p. 235; p. 321: Studio Atlantis; p. 325: Rosewood
Frank O. Gehry. Getty Research Institute, Los Angeles (2107.M 66), Frank Gehry Papers: p. 288
Michael Gluck: p. 325: C+C
Peter Grueneisen: p. 14; p. 17; p. 25; p. 28; p. 62 top; p. 87; p. 105 bottom; p. 114 top; p. 136 top; p. 196; p. 241; p. 242; p. 250; p. 251; p. 280; p. 282 top; p. 311; p. 318: Palmer; Levels; Green Roof; Manhattan Beach Pier; NPR West; Monmouth; p. 319: Skyline; Crestwood Hills; p. 320: GSN; p. 321: DMB; p. 324: Brandon's Way; Costa del Sol; p. 325: 525 Post; Larmar
gta Archiv/ETH Zürich, Hans Brechbühler: p. 15
Luc Hautecoeur: p. 324: Mega
Juergen Nogai: front cover; p. 23; p. 30; p. 32; p. 39; p. 41; p. 42/43; p. 44 bottom; p. 46 bottom; p. 50 bottom; p. 51; p. 57; p. 58/59; p. 60; p. 61; p. 62 bottom; p. 63; p. 64; p. 65; p. 66/67; p. 68; p. 69; p. 70; p. 71; p. 72; p. 73; p. 74; p. 101; p. 102; p. 103; p. 104; p. 105 top; p. 108/109; p. 111; p. 112/113; p. 114 bottom; p. 118; p. 121; p. 122; p. 123; p. 130; p. 133; p. 134; p. 135; p. 136 bottom; p. 137; p. 138; p. 139; p. 140; p. 143; p. 144; p. 145; p. 146/147; p. 148; p. 149; p. 150; p. 151; p. 152; p. 153; p. 154; p. 155; p. 156; p. 157; p. 158; p. 159; p. 160; p. 163; p. 164; p. 165; p. 166; p. 167; p. 170; p. 173; p. 174; p. 175; p. 176; p. 177; p. 181; p. 182; p. 183; p. 184 bottom; p. 188/189; p. 201; p. 202; p. 203; p. 204; p. 205; p. 206; p. 209; p. 210; p. 211; p. 212/213; p. 214; p. 239; p. 245; p. 246; p. 247; p. 248; p. 249; p. 254; p. 257; p. 258/259; p. 260; p. 261; p. 273; p. 274; p. 275; p.281; p. 283; p. 296 bottom left; p. 302 bottom; p. 304 bottom left; p. 317: Momentum; p. 318: Molino; The Barn; p. 319: Windmark; RCP1523/1551; The Farm; DreamWorks; Edinburgh; Stanford; 740 Sound; CityTV; Dakota; p. 320: Art Institute; RCP 1531/1542/1547; RCP 1537; JNH Studios; p. 322: Via de la Paz
Obayashi Corporation: p. 194
Ansel Olson: p. 217; p. 218; p. 219; p. 220; p. 320: Red Amp
Volker Kreidler: p. 290
Kazumi Kurigami/Camel: p. 323: Sony
Grant Ramaley: p. 325: Bad Animals
Sharon Risedorph: p. 83
A. Savin, WikiCommons: p. 289
Shari Schroder: p. 320: Fox DVD
Julius Shulman and Juergen Nogai: p. 35; p. 36; p. 40; p. 44 top; p. 46 top; p. 49; p. 50 top; p. 54
Shochiku: p. 265; p. 266; p. 267; p. 268/269; p. 270; p. 318: Shochiku
J. Scott Smith: p. 110; p. 322: Pennsylvania
Taiyo Watanabe: p. 88; p. 89; p. 90; p. 91; p. 92/93; p. 94; p. 95; p. 96; p. 97; p. 98; p. 168; p. 169; p. 293; p. 294/295; p. 296 top, bottom right; p. 297; p. 289/299; p. 300; p. 301; p. 302 top; p. 303; p. 304 top; p. 306; p. 318: Elbo; American Legion; West Valley
Joshua White: p. 193 top; p. 234; p. 324: Chautauqua; p. 325: The Record Plant; p. 325: Post Logic
James Wilson: p. 323: Luminous
Dita Vollmond: p. 117
Scot Zimmerman: p. 324: Counterpoint

IMPRINT

Concept: Peter Grueneisen
Editors: Michael Webb, Patricia Kot
Graphic Design: Eliana Dominguez,
Robert Andrade, Seth Ferris
Project management: Annette Gref
Production: Amelie Solbrig
Layout and typesetting: Harald Pridgar
Paper: Condat matt Périgord, 135 g/m²
Printing: optimal media GmbH, Röbel/Müritz

Library of Congress Control Number: 2020931267

Bibliographic information published
by the German National Library
The German National Library lists this publication
in the Deutsche Nationalbibliografie; detailed
bibliographic data are available on the Internet at
http://dnb.dnb.de.

ISBN 978-3-0356-2169-3

e-ISBN (PDF) 978-3-0356-2170-9

P.O. Box 44, 4009 Basel, Switzerland
Part of Walter de Gruyter GmbH, Berlin/Boston

9 8 7 6 5 4 3 2 1
www.birkhauser.com